20 Things You Must Know to Write a Great Screenplay

by Rick Reichman

Published by Central Ave. Press

© September 2008 by Rick Reichman

All rights reserved.

Requests to make copies of any part of the work should be mailed to the following address:
Central Ave. Press 8400 Menaul Blvd. NE, Suite 211-A
Albuquerque, NM 87112

ISBN 13: 978-0-9715344-7-6

Library of Congress Cataloging-in-Publication Data

Reichman, Rick, 1946-
  20 things you must know to write a great screenplay / by Rick Reichman.
    p. cm.
    ISBN 978-0-9715344-7-6 (pbk.)
  1. Motion picture authorship. I. Title. II. Title: Twenty things you must know to write a great screenplay.

PN1996.R423 2007
808.2'3--dc22

2007031422

Book cover by Kyle Zimmerman
Book design by Dugan Holt

Central Ave. Press
2132-A Central SE #144, Albuquerque, NM 87106
www.centralavepress.com

Printed in the United States of America

Acknowledgements

I would like to thank the following people for their help and assistance on this book:

Jean Riley Burnett for her editing and critique of the book proposal, critical book chapter, and for her encouragement.

James F. Boyle, my professor at the University of Southern California for teaching me the structure and format of screenwriting.

John Oelfke, my publisher at Central Avenue Press and editor and friend, who did a tremendous job of editing this book.

Barbara Jacksha, for her help in the initial editing and for allowing us to use her terrific screenplay, "True Magic", in the book.

Suzanne Spletzer, for recommending me to Central Avenue Press and for her help and encouragement.

Marcia Lee, for her invaluable assistance in editing this book.

All My Students, for teaching me so much about writing, teaching, and filmscripts.

Contents

Introduction	**11**
Why you should buy this book	11
Chapter 1: I Second That Emotion	**13**
Chapter 2: Making the Scene	**19**
Chapter 3: Scenes Are What It's All About	**25**
Bridging In	25
Conflict	27
Person vs. Self	28
Person vs. Non-human Entity	29
Person vs. Other Persons	30
Set Up	30
Characterization	31
Exposition	34
Backstory	35
Locales	35
Relationships	35
Time	36
Reversal	38
Bridging out	38
Analyzing the Scene	39
Contact Point	39
Chapter 4: Fortune of Reversals	**41**
A Reversal Must Change the Direction of a Scene	46
A Reversal Changes the Emotions of the Audience and/or One or More Characters in the Scene	46
A Reversal Must Be a Surprise — But a Logical Surprise — to the Audience and/or at Least One of the Main Characters in the Scene	47

A Reversal Must Have an Impact on What Follows	48
A Reversal Must Make the Audience Anxious to Learn What Happens Next	49

Chapter 5: Format and Everyone Else   57

Chapter 6: Formatting Your Screenplay   65

Slug Lines	65
Direction	67
Dialogue	68
Character Cue	68
Speech	68
Parentheticals	69
Fades and Cuts	69
Fades	69
Fade In	69
Fade Out	70
Cuts	70
Cut To	70
Match Cut	71
Marginals	72
Title	72
The End	72
Pagination	73
Continued	73
Using Continued	74
Generic Slugs	74
Series of Shots	75
Montage	75
SPFX	75
SFX	75
POV	75
Back to Scene	75
Wider View	75

Split Screen	75
Intercutting	75
INT./EXT.	75
Abbreviations and Caps	76
Other Capitalization Rules	77
Binding	78

Chapter 7: The Good, the Bad, and the Blind Date — 81
- Dramatic Protagonist — 82
- Dramatic Antagonist — 82

Chapter 8: A Hero is More Than a Sandwich (It's Also More Than a Beefcake) — 93

Chapter 9: Building Character — 97
- Checklist — 101
  - Character Details — 101
  - Appearance — 102
  - Back Story — 102
  - Present (Main Character) — 102
  - Motivations — 103
  - What Are Characters? — 103
  - Character Page — 104

Chapter 10: Acting Out — 107
- Three-Act Structure — 107
  - The Three Acts — 108
    - Act I - Introduction — 108
    - Act II - Problems — 109
    - Act III - Resolution — 112
  - Summary — 118

Chapter 11: Act Reversals — 121
- Act Reversals — 122
  - What is an Act Reversal? — 122

First Act Reversal	**122**
Option 1 - The Protagonist Makes a Decision	124
Option 2 - A Decision is Made for the Protagonist	125
Option 3 - The First Significant Meeting Between the Protagonist and Antagonist	125
Second Act Reversal	**128**
Chapter 12: Turn, Turn, Turn	**131**
Script Contact Point (The Opening)	131
First Contact Point	132
Normal Mode	132
First Scene Reversal	133
Story Set Point	135
Middle Reversal	136
Resolution and Ending	138
Chapter 13: Small Packages	**141**
Low Point	141
Baring the Soul	142
Climax	143
Chapter 14: Can We Talk? Part I	**145**
How and When to Use Dialogue	146
A-B Dialogue	147
Chapter 15: Can We Talk? Part II	**153**
Dialogue Surgery	153
Ten Most Common Dialogue Glitches	157
1. Too Obvious	158
2. Too Choppy	158
3. Too Repetitious, Too Repetitious, Too Repetitious	158
4. Tooooooo Long	159
5. Too Similar	160
6. Too Stilted, Artificial, or Bookish	160
7. Too Preachy	160

8. Too Introspective	161
9. Too False	162
10. Too Unbelievable (People just don't talk like that.)	162

Chapter 16: Rhythm and Rhyme and Harmony — 165
    Rhyming — 166
    Connectives — 169
    Pacing — 170
    Ellipses — 171
    Subplots — 173
    Subtext — 175

Chapter 17: First Things First — 179
    Initial Considerations — 180
        Time/Location (place) — 180
        Genre — 182
        Major Character Introduction — 184
        Dialogue — 184
    Overture — 186
        Themes — 186
        Foreshadowing — 189

Chapter 18: First Things First: The Sequel — 191
    Attitudes — 191
        Author's Attitude — 191
        Main Character's Attitude — 192
        Community Attitude — 192
    Page Pattern — 193
        Pacing — 193
        Ellipses — 194
        Idea Balance — 194
        Placement — 195
    Scene Elements — 195
        Contact Point — 195
        Conflict — 195

Characterization	196
Emotion	197
First Scene Reversal	197
People Who Need People	198
People	198
Others	198
Planning Ahead	198
Rhyming and Connectives	199
Destiny and Foreshadowing	199
The Next Scene	199
Character Arc	200
Character Facades	200
A-B Dialogue	200
Energy	201
Finale	201
First Scene Requirements	202

Chapter 19: Information, Education, and Stepping Stones   205

Books, Magazines, Newsletters	206
Classes, Workshops, Schools, Conferences	207
Critique Services, Fee Readers	209
Critique Groups	211
Contests	212

Chapter 20: Hollywood Script Structure   217

Appendix A: Movies Mentioned in Book

Appendix B: Glossary

Appendix C: Sample Screenplay

Appendix D: Suggested Reading List

Introduction

Structure determines the fate of your screenplay. Does each scene offer a surprise, a twist, or an unexpected event? Do the seven major turning points in the screenplay actually move the protagonist toward his goal? Does the dialogue produce the purposeful miscommunication that each character in your screenplay must achieve? Does the protagonist change, and does the ending really confirm that the change in the protagonist is permanent?

This book is not about theory (though there is some theory in its pages) as there are many excellent books about screenwriting theory available. This book isn't about giving you just a few good hints and then telling you to find and read other screenplays. (Reading screenplays is a helpful exercise that will reinforce and add to what you will learn in this book.) This book isn't about giving you one set of guidelines but then hedge by claiming that each film has its own set of dynamics which change as the story develops. Indeed, some successful Hollywood films break a rule or two now and then, but the vast majority of them generally adhere to the guidelines contained within these pages.

What this book will do is help you plan your script by understanding the elements that must go into each scene, each act, and finally, into your entire screenplay. Each chapter will provide you with insight into how to shape scenes that will have a maximum impact on your audience. The chapters on character development present ways to bring your characters to life and achieve the necessary changes that advance your plot. In delving into the three-act structure, this book pinpoints

1. The seven critical turning points and the contact point (opening) in the script

2. What each critical point must achieve

3. How including these seven points will propel your story from PAGE ONE to THE END

I also provide dialogue exercises to help you create characters that not only *walk the walk* but *talk the talk*, and techniques to help you arrange your plot and characters to create the story you want and the drama it must contain.

The first four chapters detail the vital building blocks for writing superb scenes. The next fourteen chapters focus on producing fantastic format, character development, three-act framework, film-speak (dialogue), parallels, pace, harmony, and openings. At the end, you'll find tips to help you polish and prepare your script for market.

This book is all about structure. It details how to create the most successful screenwriting structure that exists — which I have labeled the *Hollywood Script Structure* — and presents a concrete, step-by-step approach for applying it to your script. Whether you're writing your first script or your tenth, this system is the best one I know for organizing your ideas while allowing your creativity to flourish. Years of teaching successful students have proven to me that regardless of what kinds of screenplays you plan to pen, the way to start is by using the Hollywood Script Structure. Understanding it will provide you with a clear insight and a solid blueprint for creating exciting, engaging, and marketable screenplays.

Chapter 1
I Second That Emotion

The most important element of a film is Secondary Emotion.

What are the three most important factors of a successful film?

What is it that keeps you in your seat, or on the edge of it, ready to scream, sigh, laugh, hide your eyes, shiver, or jump? What makes you drive to the theater, hunt for a parking space, and stand in line to view a ninety to one hundred and twenty minute film? What motivates you to spend a small fortune on a Saturday night to sit in an overcrowded, uncomfortable, sometimes dirty and noisy auditorium with hundreds of other people you would normally want to avoid?

The answer is EMOTION, EMOTION, and EMOTION. Emotion is what makes a movie effective and a screenplay compelling. For us screenwriters our script is our movie and the reader our audience. So if our audience finds no emotional connection with our script, there will be no connection at all. *Sentience* is the key to creating not only good films but terrific film scripts. It's what separates the good from the great, the merely clever from the truly brilliant, the *still floating around town* from the *coming to a theater near you*.

As early as 1916, film analysts recognized the importance of the quintessential element of emotion. In that year, Hugo Munsterberg, one of the most noted film analysts of the early twentieth century, in his book *The Film: A Psychological Study* wrote that while cinema technology would vastly change, what attracted audiences to film would not. The success of a movie, he said, would always depend on the emotional reaction of the audience.

Munsterberg discussed two types of emotional responses: The first response, *primary emotion*, he defined as the emotion portrayed by the actors. The second response, *secondary emotion*, he defined as the emotion induced in an audience.

These emotional responses do not always correlate with each other and one is far more consequential than the other. Secondary emotion is the heartbeat of a superb script, and understanding how to induce it in an audience is what will bring your script to life.

Hold it! The emotions portrayed by the actors in a film and the emotional response of the audience watching it don't have to be the same? Do you question that? Invariably someone does. If Shirley MacLaine is sobbing over something or someone on screen, it is usually a good indication that the audience should be sad or sobbing as well. But suppose Abbot and Costello are being chased by the likes of Frankenstein, the Werewolf, Dracula, or a telemarketer. Abbott and Costello may be terrified, but the audience may be laughing. Clearly, the two reactions differ.

The success or failure of your script will ultimately depend on your reader's emotional response. Everything else in your work may be perfect. You can create great characters, have a terrific plot, "give" fantastic dialogue, and prepare flawlessly structured scenes. But unless you evoke the reader's passion and push those oh-so-salient emotional buttons, your script will always be 'not suitable for our present needs.'

Have I convinced you that emotion is important? Are you thinking about the emotions you tried to project in your last screenplay? Are you questioning if you really evoked those emotions? Even if you have not yet written a script, do you remember the last film you saw and why you liked or disliked it? When you boil it all down, the bottom line is, that's right, emotion.

Where does this emotion come from? Most of us assume that if we write well and follow the rules of good storytelling, our audience will react appropriately. However, a script succeeds only if each scene carries an emotional jolt.

When writing a scene, ask yourself this question: *What emotion do I want my reader to feel?* And then choreograph your scene so your readers will be emotionally where you want them to be at its conclusion. Sure it's plastic. Sure it's scheming. Sure it's manipulative. But this is storytelling not real life (although some might argue it's both), and for storytelling, choreographing the secondary emotion is vital to the success of your screenplay.

One of my students provided an excellent example of the importance of secondary emotion. One night in class this student read an original scene that seemed, in every way, top notch. The dialogue was superb and the action and structure splendid. Yet something about it bothered me and many in the class. The class worked on the problem for a while without finding a reason or a solution. Finally, someone asked, "What emotion did you want us to feel in that scene?"

The student answered, "Oh, I was leaving that up to you." BINGO, the problem was identified. Emotion can not be "left up to the reader" or your scene will invoke nothing, or at least very little, to which the reader can respond. By not addressing the element of emotion, that student rendered the scene cool and lifeless. Despite the wonderful words and excellent structure, the entire five-or-six page scene lacked spirit and life.

When writing your scene, pick an emotion and say to yourself, *in this scene, I want my reader to feel love, hate, anger, jealousy, joy, confusion, fear, or some other specific sensation.* Of course, this is easier said than written.

After all, among the myriad emotions, some are difficult to convey, some less difficult, and others incredibly hard.

Think for a moment: What emotions are the simplest to convey? Don't be too quick to answer.

Your initial selection may have been that of sadness, but since I warned you to take your time, you reformulated. After all, "Make me cry!" is the time honored challenge a director will assign anyone claiming to be an actor or actress.

Your next choice might be laughter. But Robin Williams and Whoopi Goldberg don't get paid millions for work that just anyone can do. And unless you live and labor in Washington D.C., being funny is incredibly difficult.

What then is the answer? What causes us to shiver when sitting by a campfire at night? What emotion can everyone from a newborn to an adult readily experience? You guessed it, *fear*! We grasp it quickly. We respond. If you're in a crowded room and someone tells a joke, probably not everyone will laugh. But if someone walks in with a gun, everyone will react similarly. Ghosts, goblins, ghouls, assorted psychopaths, lobbyists, and agents are enough to terrify just about anyone. Fear is the least difficult sensation to communicate and the most popular to portray. Don't be fooled, though. Fear may be slightly easier to induce in an audience than other emotions, but it is by no means easy. The writers and filmmakers who unnerve us are no less gifted than those who make us happy, sad, or want to go out and fight for some cause. For whatever reason, many people — especially younger people — enjoy being frightened in a theater. So fear has a built-in audience. Since horror films are usually less expensive to produce, is it any wonder filmmakers create a lot more movies about *Friday the Thirteenth* than *Groundhog Day*? Notwithstanding the calendar bias, fear usually sells more popcorn, is a quicker route to the psyche, and a slightly surer path to the bank.

On the opposite end of the spectrum we encounter more complex and difficult-to-portray emotions. Nearly everyone in the film industry claims to be seeking scripts depicting love, faithfulness, friendship, and selflessness. Unfortunately, these types of scripts do not guarantee the predictable audience response found in scripts for horror or suspense films.

Extracting any emotion from a reader is a challenge, and portraying complex sentiments takes a certain amount of maturity. Many writers attempt to elicit these more mature emotions with melodrama, hackneyed tricks, or overwriting. Such ruses rarely work. You must arrange your words, visuals, and content so the reader feels she's encountering true life — or at least true life within the world you've created on paper. Once a reader suspects she's being manipulated, she will almost always rebel. And that rebellion will mean the rejection of your screenplay.

I field many questions about scenes in my screenwriting classes. These are two of the most commonly asked:

Are there specific ways to control and elicit the desired emotions without being obvious?

If yes, can these techniques be learned and mastered?

The answer to the first question is *absolutely*. And the answer to the second is that learning and mastering these techniques is essentially what I teach in this book.

A screenwriter must seamlessly integrate thousands of different elements in order to write a successful screenplay. But getting a moviegoer to invest time, effort, and money in seeing a film begins with the three most important factors of movie making: EMOTION, EMOTION, and EMOTION.

Chapter 2
Making the Scene

Scene structure is the key to creating a great script.

How do we begin writing a screenplay? Most of us have a general idea of how we want our story to progress and what roles we want our characters to play. That's the simple part. But what happens next?

Most screenwriting professionals recommend beginning the script process with an outline. There are several types: You can create a prose outline that simply explains the plot, or create a brief chronological summary of the major turning points in the story — what in television is called a beat sheet. But I find that the best screenplay outline is the scene-by-scene skeleton placed on 3 x 5 or 5 x 7 index cards.

A scene card outline works especially well for the modern script because it approaches the screenplay from its basic unit, the scene.

First, we have to learn what a scene is. The following definition is taken from my first book, *Formatting Your Screenplay*:

... a segment of your screenplay (usually between 3.5 to 7 pages long) centered on a theme and/or action and having a beginning, middle, climax, and end.

The average scene will contain five or six pages of text, with each page correlating to approximately one minute of actual screen time. Thus, a 110 to 120 page script will contain approximately eighteen to twenty-five of these units strung together. Each of these units is a little story in and of itself; it has a beginning, middle, climax, and end. If a reader were to read each unit separately, she should be able to follow each scene and understand what was happening even if all the reasons and/or consequences of the action were found in other scenes in the script. But even though each unit tells its own story, you also need to keep in mind that it must generate exciting and engaging action, move the plot forward, and integrate into the overall script.

When I discuss this part of scene structure in class, someone usually asks, "How do you handle transitions between scenes?" My answer is that you should consider a transition as either part of a previous scene or part of a future scene in the script. By making a transition part of a scene, you still have to deal with only eighteen to twenty-five units. And when writing the script, those short bridges will still be there, connecting one scene with the other.

Since the scene is the foundation of a screenplay, your first priority should be learning how to build that foundation. But the boundaries delineating the beginning, middle, and end of a scene are not always easy to pinpoint. You might not know how to label a scene if it extends over long periods of film time — as opposed to real time — or how to define a scene if there are two or more points of action occurring simultaneously, or if parts of a scene are broken up by other scenes. The problem, then, is how to know when to call a scene a scene.

The first act of *Men In Black* provides us with a good example of how scenes are structured. I will briefly describe each scene, and then place the scene length in parentheses.

The movie begins with an *overture* (2:36). (A film overture, which we'll discuss in much greater detail in chapters 17 and 18, is generally the first few pages of the script, written so that all the themes of the film are hinted at by the various visuals and/or dialogue of the characters.) Then we're introduced to Kay and his partner Dee as they hunt down a fugitive alien (6:46). Next, we see James Edwards chasing and cornering a bizarre "perp" (3:00). After we're introduced to

The Bug — soon to be Edgar The Bug — we return to the police station (3:25).

At the police station, James explains his strange chase to the police inspector. Immediately afterwards, James and Kay meet and then visit Jack Jeebs. The section ends with Kay and James finishing a meal at a restaurant (6:03).

In a short segment, Edgar The Bug "takes care" of a pest exterminator (1:10). And the seventh and last section of the first act shows Zed testing James to determine his suitability as new partner for Kay (7:04).

As you can see, Act I of *Men In Black* balances short sections and long ones. Now let's look at how these sections come together as scenes.

I'll focus on overture in chapters 17 and 18. For now, let's start with James' introduction. His chase consumes three minutes of screen time and could conceivably count as a scene that's half a minute short, or it could be combined with the time it takes him to explain to the police inspector what happened during the chase (5:17).

If the latter option is chosen, then the first meeting between Kay and James would count as a separate scene (4:48).

By combining Edgar The Bug's introduction with the short segment where Edgar gets rid of the pest exterminator, we get (5:36), even though these two segments are split by the long passage containing James' explanation to the police inspector, and by James' and Kay's first meeting.

The final section of the first act is a definitive scene that begins when James shows up at MIB Headquarters. The middle part shows James taking several tests, the climax occurs when Kay picks James as his new partner.

These time sequence scenarios show, in a roundabout way, that scenes are what you interpret them to be. What one person considers a complete scene, I might not, and vice-versa. Neither are necessarily right or wrong, and it's not critical that you pinpoint precisely where each scene belongs in say, *Chinatown*, *You Can Count on Me*, *The Aviator*, or *Men In Black*. As you can see from the *Men In Black* example, sometimes scenes are precise and sometimes they aren't. What is important is that you learn to cultivate a sense of what a scene is, and learn how to develop scenes that work for your own writing and for your own scripts.

Recognizing scene structure may seem complex and difficult at first, but there are ways to make it easier. Practice singling out scenes from your favorite films, and then review your own script and put together four-to-seven page segments that have a beginning, middle, climax, and end, and are centered on a theme and/or action. The more you practice, the easier it gets. Once you're able to create your own scenes, you'll have less difficulty putting together the eighteen to twenty-five you need to complete your screenplay.

Fortunately, we screenwriters have some guidelines for creating dynamic scenes.

1. An effective scene consists of seven major elements, which we'll discuss in greater detail in the next chapter.

    Bridging In
    Conflict
    Set up
    Characterization
    Exposition
    Reversal
    Bridging Out

2. Each one of these elements must be in the scene or the scene will fail.

3. Each scene has a contact point — a correct place to begin. If your contact point begins too early, your scene will bore the reader, and if it starts too late, it may confuse him.

4. Each scene must advance the story. It's not enough to show only the quirkiness of some character or impart information or bandy great dialogue. A scene may do all of these, but if it does nothing to advance the story, then it should either be rewritten or abandoned.

5. Each scene must project some emotional quality.

I champion the scene and its structure as the basic component of the script for three reasons: First, it's easier to identify and write a defined, cohesive unit than it is to struggle with numerous smaller pieces. Second, for many screenwriters, this highly arranged system can actually enhance creativity. I've witnessed a number of students who over-described their settings, revealed too much about their characters, or lacked punch in their action, turn their scenes around once they learned the elements that make a bland scene great. And finally, understanding scene structure makes it much easier to identify and correct the inevitable challenges that arise when writing your script.

Chapter 3
Scenes Are What It's All About

Every scene must include the seven critical elements and a clear contact point.

It's on a bumper sticker I see occasionally, *Maybe the Hokey-Pokey is what it's all about.* In a screenplay, the scene is what it's all about. You put certain elements in, you take overwriting out, you make sure there's a reversal, and then you get out. By learning the dance steps that comprise a scene you learn how to create the structure and style each scene must possess. And it's that structure and style that helps you develop the secondary emotion every scene needs in order to succeed.

As I discussed in Chapter 2, every well-written scene contains seven elements and a clear contact point. Let's examine each element and then the contact point.

Bridging In

Bridging in opens your scene and consists of a *slug line* and the prose paragraph that follows. Slug lines (hereafter referred to as slugs) are those always-capitalized single entries that look like this:

EXT. RESTAURANT - DAY

When opening a scene, you will almost always follow the slug with a prose paragraph that introduces a situation, presents characters, or describes some object or action. Beginning a scene with dialogue when the audience doesn't know who is in the scene or what the scene is about is risky at best.

As with all direction (prose) paragraphs, always keep the first scene paragraph short, no more than four lines. So the bridging in might appear like this:

EXT. MANHATTAN STREET/SOHO - DUSK

Lights from towers, shops, apartments, and lofts transform the city streets from the business of the day to the life of the night.

Your scene opening can cover up to one-ninth — or slightly more than an inch — of the page. And in that space, you must accomplish several tasks:

1. Specify the time and location, normally in the slug.

2. Set the tone. Is it breezy, funny, deadly serious, dark, or dramatic? Make your words convey how you want the scene to feel to the reader. This "feeling" is the first indication of the emotional content of your scene.

3. Introduce a place, character, situation, and/or object.

4. Create a sense of style and pace that influences how the reader connects with the material.

5. Engage the reader enough so that she's anxious to find out what happens as the scene progresses.

Is your scene description interesting enough to entice your reader to delve deeper into your story? If you open with characters, are they important or influential enough to emotionally engage the reader? And most importantly, does your scene open in a place that won't confuse or bore your reader? If your opening meets these criteria, then your bridging in is probably on target.

Because you have so little physical space to bridge in effectively, each word you write must be absolutely necessary to the scene and transmit as much information as possible. Your words and phrases must quickly convey the tone, pace, and visual(s) that frame the next four-to-seven pages of your scene. Economy of language is always important to a script, but in scene openings especially, the right words, phrases, or sentences will determine whether the reader yawns or fawns over what happens next.

Conflict

Without conflict there is no drama. Without drama there is no story. Two or more people simply getting along may be nice, but that isn't what gets your script playing in a theater near you.

Emotional tension created by conflict holds an audience's interest. Real-life events offer the best proof of that. In 1989, the Berlin Wall — a potent symbol of Communism — was torn down. It was an historic event, and one that most of us had hoped to someday witness. When we got our wish, CNN covered nearly every minute of the happy celebration on and near the wall. How did that affect CNN's ratings? The Nielsens reflected almost no change.

You want ratings? Tiananmen Square, huge numbers; Persian Gulf Wars, an absolute smash; celebrity trials, gargantuan numbers. We're drawn to events that involve conflict. We become involved and emotionally connected. Conflict is what keeps us watching that sporting event, trial, or soap opera instead of cleaning the dishes, finishing that report for work, or working on our screenplay. Keep your reader engaged by building conflict into each scene you write.

Just what is conflict? Someone once described it as two dogs, one bone. It's the fight over the watering hole in *2001: A Space Odyssey*, the gentle, verbal disagreements in *My Dinner With Andre*, fighting a killer android in *Terminator*, and a wrenching life-and-death decision in *Million Dollar Baby*. Each is conflict, and conflict used well.

In *My Dinner With Andre*, Wally discusses his new electric blanket and how much he likes it even though it changes his sleeping patterns. Andre answers that he would never want or use an electric blanket because having an electric blanket cuts one off from the real world — a world where it's cold and you have sympathy for others who are cold. Okay, so it ain't "Are you feeling lucky, punk?" but it is conflict. And conflict is what makes a movie work.

There are three major categories of conflict:

1. Person vs. Self

2. Person vs. Non-human Entity (Nature, God, Technology, Monsters, Spirits, etc.)

3. Person vs. Other Person(s)

Person vs. Self is easily portrayed in prose or plays. In novels or short stories, we describe the thoughts and images in a character's mind as unspoken dialogue. In a play the characters are allowed soliloquy, which, for good reason, is rare in movies. So how do you portray an interior conflict like Person vs. Self in a visual medium such as a movie?

Difficult, isn't it? The right actor can help, but there's no guarantee that the best actor for your character will be cast. Casting is a tricky business at best, and Hollywood is replete with true stories about actors and actresses who were supposed to have played certain roles in particular movies. The list includes

Bette Davis as Scarlett O'Hara in *Gone With The Wind*
Ronald Reagan as Rick Blaine in *Casablanca*

Tom Selleck as Indiana Jones in *Raiders Of The Lost Ark*
Sylvester Stallone as Axel Foley in *Beverly Hills Cop*

Think of how different those films would have been had those casting choices actually happened.

So now we return to the original question: *How do you show internal conflict?* *Superman III* tried to present Person vs. Self in a literal sense when the audience witnessed a clash between Clark Kent and Superman. For me, that attempt to visualize internal conflict failed. It seemed a little too obvious, like presenting subtext when text would have worked so much better. It does work, however, in *Dr. Jekyll and Mr. Hyde,* as well as in some of its reincarnations such as *The Nutty Professor, The Mask,* etc.

Person vs. Self is difficult though not impossible to portray visually. But because at least one of your characters, the protagonist, must undergo change and therefore internal conflict, internal conflict must be a part of every screenplay.

What about *Person vs. Non-human Entity*? In *The Matrix* and *Men In Black,* reality must be kept from the citizenry. In *War Games,* David must stop Joshua — the computer's Global Thermal Nuclear War Game — from initiating World War Three. Nothing can be more terrifying than the impending annihilation of the planet. This is extraordinary conflict.

Of course, non-human entities can also be computers, creepy-crawly aliens, ghouls, goblins, or politicians. *Castaway* and *The Perfect Storm* depict Person against Nature. *Agnes of God* and *Dogma* dramatize Person vs. Religion and Person vs. God. *Godzilla* portrays Person vs. Monster, and *Godzilla vs. Bambi* is. . .oh well, you can see that one for yourself.

Many times, when there is conflict between a person and non-human entity, the writer anthropomorphizes the entity by making it more human or human-like. Screenwriters have humanized a mule (Francis), a horse (Mr. Ed), a computer (HAL in *2001: A Space Odyssey*), God(s) (*Oh God* and *Clash of the Titans*), angels (*Dogma*), ghosts (*Ghost*), the devil (*Oh God, You Devil*), automobiles (*Christine* and *Herbie: The Love Bug*), and even the biggest horror, Hollywood agents. Arguably, conflict with human-like animals and objects may actually belong in our third group: *Person vs. Other Persons*.

Whether it's Rambo taking on the North Vietnamese or Soviet armies in the *First Blood* sequels, or George battling Mr. Potter in *Bedford Falls*, conflict with others gives the writer access to the full range of visual and emotional discord. Person vs. Other Person(s) is easily understood, and the writer can more naturally create secondary emotion when one person interacts with another.

Conflict is what keeps your characters motivated and your audience emotionally involved. It is crucial to the success of any good screenplay. You must include at least one of the three types of conflict in each scene. Of course, if you can include two or even all three types in each scene, so much the better. Just make sure to generate conflict in every scene, page, and piece of prose or dialogue in your screenplay.

Set Up

A magician focuses your attention toward stage right where you expect a tiger to appear from out of nowhere, while at the same time he makes an elephant appear from behind him. *Set up* has a similar function. It acts as a red herring, misleading your audience as to where your scene is headed.

If John Wayne rides into town seeking the "toughest guy" around, the viewer expects to see a fight. If a close family has a reunion, we expect to see them sharing wonderful moments from the past. And if character A chases character B, we anticipate A will capture B sometime, somewhere along the way.

Mislead your audience by providing them some seemingly obvious clues that lead them to believe they're one step ahead of you. But if you, the magician, the entertainer, the one with the big bag of tricks, construct the set up effectively, the surprises and shifts that take place later in the scene will be logical but, as much as possible, unexpected.

Characterization

Getting to know and understand characters is one of the most important aspects of connecting with a movie. Your audience must be emotionally invested in your characters in order to have an emotional connection with your story. You keep your audience interested in your characters by slowly and methodically revealing their intentions and personality. Portraying characters in a script is like eating an artichoke. You peel away one leaf at a time. You savor it. You peel the next leaf, and the next, until you reach the heart.

The best way to expose your characters' personalities is by letting your audience learn just a little more about them in each scene in which they appear. Be aware though, that a character may appear in a scene in various ways.

1. A character appears when he or she is physically present in the scene. It doesn't matter how long or in what capacity the character is there; if he or she plays any kind of role in the scene, we should learn a little something more about him or her.

A character also appears

2. If others in the scene mention that particular individual

3. If someone or something in the scene represents him or her (the character's car or a painting created by the character)

4. If the character is on a tape or film played in the movie itself

5. If we see manifestations of the character, such as her ghost or holograph

6. If there's an oblique reference to a place, object, or incident that directly relates to a character

In *Romancing the Stone,* the drug lord — a big fan of Joan Wilder who helps Joan and Jack escape — appears in the first act. Remember when Joan and her agent talk in Joan's apartment just before she leaves for South America? The agent tells Joan that her books sell best in South America. Bingo! a parenthetical introduction of the drug lord long before he makes a physical appearance in the film.

I repeat, the audience should learn a little something more about a character each time he appears. Many writers make the mistake of presenting full resumes for their characters as soon they materialize. There's no reason that lengthy histories and psychologies of any of your characters need appear in your script. Remember, this isn't a job interview; the character already has the job.

Keep in mind that when a character appears in your scene, most of the space on the page needs to be filled with doing, not explaining. We learn a little bit more than we knew about the character, and that helps us understand what she does, how she reacts, and what motivates her both in the scene and in the remaining story.

Don't forget that you have the entire script in which to present your characters' backstory, motivations, and nature. For your minor characters, a few details usually suffice.

In *Chinatown*, for instance, we don't need to know on page one that Jake Gittes was a cop, that he quit the force, or that he tried to help someone who got killed in Chinatown. We have the rest of the film to learn that information. On the other hand, we never need to know that much about Curly, the man in the office viewing the pictures. He appears only twice, and we learn from him only what's important to the story.

In *Million Dollar Baby*, we get to know Maggie through her actions and Scrap's narrative. Even though Maggie's family plays a large role in the film, we see them only twice. We learn about Maggie's family by witnessing her sacrifices for them as well as by hearing about them through her dialogue. So finally, when Maggie tells her family how she feels about the "contract" they want her to sign, we cheer her on.

Audiences like character surprises. Show the shark in *Jaws* at the beginning of the film and the audience will get up, go home, and tell their friends not to see the movie. Show the shark later, after you've built up how big, powerful, and terrifying it is, and moviegoers will have a lot more fun seeing if their own imaginations match what ultimately appears on the screen. (Not to mention that you get to use a great line about needing a bigger boat.)

How do you determine how much character development to provide in any one scene? Ask yourself how much the viewer needs to know at any particular point, how much is necessary to advance the plot, and how much is necessary to further develop or reveal your character.

Remember, characterization is best shown through your characters' actions. If your character is doing well, has a lover, a great job, and his ball club is headed toward a championship, we tend to think that he's probably a pretty decent (albeit boring) guy. But turn all those factors around by having his lover leave, his job sour, and his team lose in the playoffs, and then see how interesting he becomes. How does he fight back? What does he do that keeps him treading water instead of being pulled under? Film is a visual medium, and character and character change — like most everything else in a movie — must be conveyed through visuals.

Exposition

Exposition is information that the audience must know in order to understand the scene. Exposition helps the reader understand what is happening in the scene, and, like characterization, is provided a little at a time on a need-to-know basis.

Mise-en-Scene is a French term meaning everything in the frame, how it is placed, and how that placement has an emotional impact on the audience. Anything — and usually everything — in a frame is there to provide us with information. So make sure that the words you choose create an aura of how you see the setting, the characters, and the situation. Make sure your depiction of the scene conveys all the flavor, mystery, energy, ambience, and drama that it's possible to convey. Make sure that every written shot in your script is exactly what you want and need to move your reader.

Over the years, moviemakers have tried to enhance the film-watching experience by using gimmicks both in and out of frame. *Odorama* — the placing of scents in the air ducts of the theater to draw an audience's response — did not prove popular with those who had allergies or other respiratory ailments.

Cinerama and *3-D* were fads for about ten days. And *Shockarama*, which consisted of electrodes placed strategically in certain seats and triggered whenever something frightening happened, was another less than delightful innovation and a real bummer for those with pace-makers or heart problems.

There are excellent methods of imparting information to an audience that don't involve trickery. These include story elements such as *backstory*, *relationships*, *locales*, and *time*. What are these elements and how are they used?

Backstory is who, what, why, and how. Who are these characters? What made them the type of people they are? How and why did they come to be where they are when our story opens? Once you've created and worked with each of your characters, you'll probably know a lot more about them than you'll ever reveal in your screenplay. However, the more you know about your characters and the more three-dimensional they become, the more real and multifaceted they will appear to the reader and audience.

Locales reveal the texture of the universe your characters inhabit. One of the first questions you must answer is *why is my story set where it's set?* It shouldn't be, *'Cause that's where I want it.* The locale you choose for your setting should reflect the people who inhabit your story and strengthen the plot of your screenplay. While not every location should have the same influence as say, Nashville had on the movie of the same name (in that case the city became as much a character in the story as the actors were), location can and does influence how people act, react, and interact.

A story set in Washington D.C., for example, poses different dynamics from a story set in Los Angeles. A drama set in the city differs from a drama in the country. A United States setting differs from a foreign setting. And in outer space there are all kinds of environments that would not be relevant on planet Earth.

Relationships help the reader interpret characters and situations in the script. Your character's relationship with relatives, friends, lovers or ex-lovers, co-workers, and casual acquaintances are all vital cues that help your audience become more involved with the people and situation(s) you create in your screenplay.

Time, too, serves as a tool for scene exposition. Historical time clues the reader into the manners, mores, and sympathies of the day. The season (and sometimes even the hour of day) clues the reader into factors such as lighting and weather. Historical time — which should always be identified at the beginning of a script — supplements the reader's knowledge regarding the coming story and frees her, and later the audience, from spending their time trying to guess "when" they are.

Despite gimmicks and technological innovation, information in today's films is presented in essentially the same way it's been presented in drama throughout the ages, by what we see and what we hear. (Even in silent films there was often theme music supplied by a piano or organ player hired by the theater.)

What do we see? We see characters, costumes, and settings which hint at the time, place, values, and type of people in our movie. We see symbols (the lions on Dennis' grave in *Out of Africa*, the green wash glove in *E.T.*, the neuralyzer in *Men In Black*, and the speed bag in *Million Dollar Baby*). We also see signs, props, titles, special effects, lighting, and even camera angles — though some of these items would never be indicated in our script.

What do we hear? We hear dialogue, narration, and voice over. We hear sound effects and music that intensify and reinforce the action or sentiments being portrayed on-screen. We hear ambient noises. Even if a character in the film is bound, gagged, and blindfolded, if he hears cars, sirens, trucks, and trains we might reasonably believe he's in a city. If he hears birds, crickets, and little else, we might deduce he's in the country. And if he hears lawn mowers, complaints about taxes, or gas grills, we'll know he's in suburbia.

Another type of exposition is provided by a modern version of the Greek chorus. A crowd of people reacting to an event they witness is a chorus. Bits and pieces of conversation from small clusters of people at a party is a chorus. Sometimes, as in *Babe, Mighty Aphrodite*, or the musical version of *Little Shop of Horrors*, a chorus is actually a chorus. A chorus hints at events about to happen, and adds to or alters the tone and mood set by the characters and story.

Obviously, the writer cannot control every facet of a motion picture — lighting, music, camera angles, and other production elements will be decided by the director and staff. But you may have more influence on the final product than you realize. It all depends on how you communicate your vision in your script.

One good way to describe a place, for instance, is to emphasize ambiance. Citing one revealing object often conveys an impression better and faster than if you detailed an entire setting. For instance, you might identify a study as macho by describing the giant, stuffed grizzly in the corner.

One difficulty with exposition that appears at the beginning of many films is what I call the *Now What* syndrome. We have all seen films that started off with an absolute BANG! They got us hooked and involved. They were screenplay minutes we would kill to write. But then. . .but then. . .the writer, remembering he must tell us what the heck this movie is about, imparts the information via too many minutes of nothing but *talking heads* (successive pages of dialogue with little or no action) and our interest and emotional involvement wanes.

Several strategies can help you avoid the *Now What* syndrome. James Bond usually learns his new assignment quickly and then amuses himself and the audience by playing with the new technology he'll be using. After Indiana Jones' adventure in the cave in *Raiders of the Lost Ark*, Messrs. Kasdan and Spielberg use the antics of the young women in the classroom to add some humor to the film while we learn more about Indy. What follows next is a short but fascinating history lesson which is directly tied to the plot and prepares us for Indy's newest adventure.

Information, like good seasoning in food, must be sprinkled in carefully, a little at a time. Seasonings should be subtle, but the food would be bland without them. Without the skillful use of exposition, your screenplay will be either unintelligible or tiresome.

Reversal

A *reversal* is the point in a scene at which the action and/or emotion (secondary and primary) either takes a surprising twist or reaches an unexpected intensity.

You plan your scene like a magician. You make the reader think he knows what is about to happen. But he doesn't know until it happens. The *does* point is reversal.

Reversals are so important that I have devoted the entire next chapter to them. For now, suffice it to say, reversals are the most critical elements in screenplays. They provide the surprises in a script; they push the story forward. They are the pulse and emotional high-points of a script. With them, your script can sparkle, shine, and light up a room. Without them. . .it's just another dull day at the computer.

Bridging out

To *Bridge out* means to exit the scene. The question is *when to say when?* You can linger too long and bore your reader, or you can stop short and confuse him. In a sitcom, the rule is to always exit the scene on a joke. Unfortunately, no corresponding rule exists for drama or even film comedy.

One hint regarding when to bridge out is that since the reversal is a climax or turning point, it often comes near the end of the scene. So once the characters and/or audience realize that what once seemed imminent has actually changed, they should react. This audience reaction is your cue that the very next step is to get the heck out of Haiti.

Analyzing the Scene

So how do you know if you have everything that belongs in the scene? Make a list, and yes, check it twice. Do you have conflict? Is the conflict visual and affecting? Is characterization and exposition provocative, clear, and not overdone? Does your bridging in and set up provide strong but deceptive clues as to what will happen next? Do you have a reversal — climax or turning point — in the scene? Is it clear and not clichéd? Has your scene told its mini-story and advanced the plot? Did the characters and situation convey an emotional impact on your reader? Have your characters reacted to the reversal?

If the answer is yes to each question above, your scene is probably complete, and it is time to advance to a new slug.

Contact Point

As I mentioned earlier, the *contact point*, or where to open a scene, is critical to a scene's success. Remember our examples from *Men In Black*? The opening of the second scene begins with James chasing a suspect. It doesn't matter why James is chasing the man because the action speaks for itself. If we had opened earlier to see what caused James to start the chase, we would have added information that we didn't really need and slowed down an exciting incident. If we opened only moments later, when James jumps onto the double-decker bus, we wouldn't know what was happening in the scene.

The contact point should be the point in the scene at which the action begins. And the action presented should lead smoothly into the set up and ultimately to the climax (reversal) that you have planned.

To construct a terrific scene, know these seven elements so well you can recite them in your sleep. For each unit, or scene, of your script you should be able to name what emotion you want the reader to feel and describe how you will use each of the seven elements to make her feel it. Be clear what your contact point is (the beginning) and when you will bridge out of the scene (the end), and confirm that this particular scene advances your plot. Finally, make certain you have strong, clear reversals, because it is those reversals that will propel or dispel your screenplay.

Chapter 4
Fortune of Reversals

A strong and clear reversal is the key to every scene in a screenplay.

Where is the reversal?

I have asked this question so often in my classes that a student once suggested it should be my epitaph. I belabor the point because for most ineffective scenes, the reversal is weak or missing entirely.

A reversal is the scene climax. A reversal is "see change." A reversal is the magic. A reversal is the pin to which the entire scene is hooked. A reversal is what gives your scene surprise, lift, and life, and ensures that your scene and story maintains energy and momentum.

Picture a heart monitor machine. The monitor depicts a patient's heartbeat as a jagged line that at regular intervals spurts to a peak. Reversals are those peaks in your screenplay. You must include that surge, or reversal, at least every five to six pages (minutes) or your feature will flatline.

So, what is a reversal? As we learned in Chapter 3

A reversal is a point in a scene at which the action and/or emotion (secondary or primary) either takes a surprising twist or reaches an unexpected intensity.

You may not have heard the term before, yet reversal is as old as drama itself. Aristotle discusses *Peripeteia*, or reversal of the situation. In Chapter 11 of the *Poetics* he writes,

Reversal of the situation is a change by which the action veers round to its opposite, subject to our rule of probability or necessity.

The most sensational examples of reversals are found in the old Saturday morning serials that appeared in movie theaters in the late thirties through the fifties. The serials used a simple technique: At the end of each week's episode the hero would appear hopelessly trapped, but the beginning of the next feature always revealed a new angle, a part of the puzzle not seen before, that saved the day and the hero.

Have you seen anything similar recently? Sure. Stephen Spielberg and George Lucas decided to use the cliffhanger technique to create a new full-length feature film style. The result was the Indiana Jones series.

Though the Indiana Jones films may be the modern epitome of the cliffhanger, the recipes they use are not exclusive to action-adventure movies. Most every Hollywood film from *Ordinary People* to *Terminator*, from *Sleepless in Seattle* to *Silence of the Lambs*, from *Forrest Gump* to *The Matrix* to *Sideways* has numerous reversals.

Sideways, a film about two friends who take a wine-tasting trip to the California vineyard country, doesn't lend itself as naturally to reversals as do action-adventure or suspense films. Reversals, however, helped it become both a box-office and critical success.

Let's look at how some of those reversals shape this story.

Miles has planned and looked forward to this trip with his buddy Jack, but he's "experienced" enough wine the night before to produce a significant hangover and sleeps well past the time he is supposed to be on the road.

Miles surprises both Jack and his mother by stopping to see her for her birthday. Miles steals money from his mother.

Miles and Jack unexpectedly meet up with Maya, a waitress at a local restaurant whom Miles had said he was interested in dating.

Even though it's obvious that Maya would like to be with Miles that evening, Miles tells her that he and Jack are going back to the motel to crash.

Jack tells Miles that his ex, Victoria, has remarried, which sends Miles into a tailspin.

Jack meets Stephanie and sets up a double date with Miles and Maya. At dinner, even though it's obvious Maya is interested in Miles, Miles calls his ex-wife.

When Jack and Miles play golf, the foursome behind them pushes them to speed up by hitting a ball near them. Miles retaliates by hitting the ball back and banging it against the foursome's cart. Two of the players get in their cart and drive toward Jack and Miles. Jack grabs a club and, swinging it wildly, shouts at the people in the cart and scares them away.

Again, Jack sets up a double date. Miles and Maya spend the night together. The next day, Miles accidentally mentions Jack's rehearsal dinner. After further questioning, he tells Maya about Jack's wedding. Maya becomes angry with Miles for being deceitful and breaks off their relationship.

Upon learning of Jack's engagement, Stephanie attacks Jack by beating him with her motorcycle helmet and breaking his nose.

At dinner, Jack picks up a waitress named Cammi. Miles is asleep at the motel when Jack wakes him by knocking on the door. Miles opens the door to find Jack naked and shivering. Jack tells Miles that Cammi's husband came home early, and he escaped by running out of the house stark naked and then ran the several miles back to the motel.

Miles agrees to retrieve the wallet Jack left at Cammi's house. Miles grabs the wallet from inside the bedroom while Cammi and her husband are having sex. Cammi's husband chases Miles, who barely escapes.

Jack needs to provide an explanation about why his nose was broken, so he purposely crashes Miles' car.

Miles writes Maya a letter. Maya responds via telephone. Maybe there is hope for Miles yet. Miles decides to visit Maya.

Let's also look at *Forrest Gump*, another box-office success that does not, at first glance, seem as conducive to reversals as other kinds of films. The reversals in *Forrest Gump* include

The school principal denies Forrest admittance. But Forrest's mother gets him admitted to school by sleeping with the principal.

On the first day of school, Forrest is treated cruelly by everyone on the school bus and isn't allowed to sit in any of the empty seats. When it seems that Forrest will be left standing and alone, Jenny befriends him by offering him a seat next to her.

Forrest is chased by his classmates. His leg braces slow him down and it appears that he'll be caught and beaten. But his braces fall away and he escapes with astounding speed.

Forrest is being chased again. This time he escapes his tormentors by running across a high school football field during the middle of a game. Bear Bryant is scouting the game and is so astonished by Forrest's speed that he recruits him to play football for the University of Alabama.

Forrest manages to join the Army even though he would normally be prevented from doing so because of his low IQ.

Forrest escapes from danger during a battle in Vietnam. But he runs back into the jungle to save his best friend Bubba. In an ironic reversal, Forrest is able to save the lives of everyone in his squad except Bubba.

Forrest meets President Johnson at a White House ceremony. Unexpectedly, Forrest exposes the war wound on his rear to the President.

Forrest and Lieutenant Dan don't take their shrimp boat into dock during a fierce storm. As a result, they have the only shrimp boat in the area still operable.

Lieutenant Dan buys Forrest stock in what Forrest believes is a fruit company. The company is Apple Computer.

Jenny reveals that Forrest is the father of her son.

While writing a reversal into each scene is important — and you would be surprised by how many scenes written by amateur and even professionals screenwriters lack one — it is not always enough. Writing the most effective reversal possible often spells the difference between *Not bad* and *We have a deal*. An effective reversal must

1. Change the direction of the scene

2. Change the emotional reaction of the main characters in the scene and/or the audience

3. Be a surprise — but a logical surprise — to the main characters in the scene and/or the audience

4. Have an impact on what follows

5. Make the audience anxious to discover what happens next

Let's consider each of these criteria.

A reversal must change the direction of the scene.

Does the turning point change the audience's or characters' expectations about where the events in the scene are headed?

In *Raiders of the Lost Ark*, Indy finds Marian alive but bound and gagged in the Germans' tent. Both Marian and the audience expect Indy to set her free. Instead, Indy leaves her in the tent so that the Germans will continue to believe that he's dead.

In one scene from *Dead Poet's Society*, the painfully reticent Todd can barely stammer when he's called on to recite a poem in class. But under pressure and with encouragement from the teacher, Todd spontaneously creates a poem.

In *The Fugitive*, Dr. Kimball hides in his downstairs rental believing the police who have surrounded the house have come for him. But the police are there to bust the landlady's son instead.

In *The Aviator*, Howard Hughes mortgages his company to pay for the risky reshooting of his film, *Hell's Angels*, with new talking picture technology.

A reversal changes the emotions of the audience and/or one or more of the main characters in the scene.

A reversal should alter not only the direction but the mood of a scene.

Marian's joy at seeing Indy changes to protest and fear when he replaces the gag. But the audience, worried about whether Indy can release Marian before the Germans return, laughs at Indy's unexpected, but logical, action.

In Million Dollar Baby, Frankie loses his boxer, Big Willie, to another manager who promises Willie a championship bout.

In Ordinary People, Conrad's distress over standing next to his mother for a photograph escalates to rage when he shouts at his father, "Give her the Goddamn camera!" At that instant, the theater audience is as stunned as the characters in the film. This moment of unexpected intensity is evidence of the emotions the characters have been hiding just below the surface.

Not every reversal needs to be this emotionally powerful. As long as all the criteria required of a reversal are met, a phone call that interrupts an important conversation or a moment of amusement that lightens a dark situation may suffice.

A reversal must be a surprise — but a logical surprise — to the audience and/or at least one of the main characters in the scene.

Audiences who have "seen it all" might wonder if there is anything left in film that can surprise them. In *Honeymoon in Vegas*, a delightful plane load of surprises awaits Jack Singer and the audience. Jack boards a plane to Las Vegas and finds it filled with Elvis impersonators. Jack and the audience are further surprised to discover that the impersonators are members of a branch of the national Elvis Skydiving Club about to perform a jump over Las Vegas. But the scene's main reversal — the biggest surprise of all — is when Jack realizes that he too is expected to jump.

Another sensational and much parodied reversal takes place in *The Crying Game* when a former IRA member discovers that the woman he is seducing is not a woman after all. A powerful twist occurs in *The Fugitive* when a Federal Marshall tells his captive that he doesn't care whether he is guilty or innocent. And in an astonishing turn of events in *Shindler's List*, a Nazi associate in World War II Austria is persuaded to save thousands of Jewish lives.

In *Chicago*, Roxie Hart shoots and kills her lover.

In *The Sixth Sense*, after Cole Sear tells Dr. Malcolm Crowe that he sees and communicates with dead people, Malcolm diagnoses Cole as suffering from schizophrenia.

The above reversals are effective because they are unexpected. But even an action we would consider logical or normal in real life can be a good reversal if the action has rarely been seen or done in movies.

Remember when Indy shoots the swordsman in *Raiders of the Lost Ark*? Audiences have seen similar situations where the hero, facing the villain's sword, had access to a gun or rifle. But in those films the good guy never did the obvious — use the more deadly weapon to slay the enemy — because it simply was not sporting or gentlemanly. Using the gun to kill the swordsman was not in the original *Raiders of the Lost Ark* script either. This reversal purportedly happened on set, to the pleasure and surprise of everyone.

One way to achieve these clever surprises is to invent several options for your scene that change direction, turn emotions, and surprise the character(s) and even yourself. As you invent these options, always seek the unexpected — a twist that is unique to the situation. After creating several reversals, write the scene with the reversal that seems the strongest. Later, return to the scene and try to create an even stronger, more unexpected twist. It may be that the reversal you've written is the right one, or it may be that you can achieve something even stronger and more startling.

A reversal must have an impact on what follows.

A change in direction affects how the audience reacts and/or how the characters approach the next set of circumstances. Even if the reversal doesn't affect what happens in the next scene or two, it will have an influence somewhere down the line. To look at it another way, everything in a screenplay ultimately intersects and connects with the main story. If the reversal has no effect on the subsequent story, then the entire scene in which it appears is probably unnecessary. So strengthen the reversal or get rid of the scene.

A reversal must make the audience anxious to discover what happens next.

A good reversal keeps the plot from becoming predictable and propels the story and the characters into unknown and unpredictable worlds. Remember, your characters and situations will probably change to some degree as you write your script — so you must be flexible and open to that change. If you and your characters are reasonably sure where you are headed but not quite sure how you will get there, then HALLELUJAH! Maybe you and your audience are in for some terrific surprises.

In *Back to the Future*, George is ready to ask Lorraine to the dance but backs out. How will Marty change the situation? Our two heroes are captured in *Lethal Weapon*. How will they escape? In *A Little Romance*, the kids and their friend have blown their cover. How will they slip the authorities? Sammy's job is threatened in *You Can Count On Me*. How will she resolve her problem?

Reversals provide the answers to these questions. Whether by solving problems or creating new ones, reversals change the immediate situation and set the stage for the next hurdle and the next surprise.

Reversals, then, are a kind of magic. And we desire magic. We seek it in books and plays and TV and sporting events and movies every day of the year. Reversals keep us guessing which rabbit will leap from which hat. A scene that provides us with a provocative twist makes us eager for the next scene — the next piece of enchantment to follow.

Fine, you say, a reversal belongs in every scene. But, you wonder, *where in the scene does the reversal go?* The answer is the same place an eight-hundred pound gorilla sleeps — anywhere it wants to.

Though it usually materializes near the end, a reversal may appear anywhere in the scene. A scene begins with the bridging in and travels in a certain direction (set up). The audience is drawn into the scene as the conflict builds and the stakes mount. They think they know where the scene is headed and the climax that awaits them. But just before the end of the scene...*BOOM!* The reversal hits, the direction changes, the emotions shift, the story line alters, and the audience waits to discover where this new event will lead.

A superb reversal occurs just before the end of a scene in *The Silence of the Lambs*. While Clarice is in the town in Ohio where Buffalo Bill killed his first victim, FBI agents prepare to storm a house just outside of Chicago where they (and the audience) believe Buffalo Bill will be found. The camera and audience focus on the ringing doorbell as Buffalo Bill answers the door. But instead of F.B.I. agents, we see Clarice alone at the door of the Ohio house — the house where Buffalo Bill actually lives. We barely have time to catch our collective breath before she steps inside.

A reversal also comes near the end of a scene in *Beetle Juice*. A car swerves to avoid running over a dog and plunges into a river. The dog watches, barks, and the scene ends.

Reversals also can occur at other points in a scene. In *War Games*, a major reversal actually ends a scene as well as the second act. David and his girlfriend are being chased when a military helicopter suddenly appears. They try to hide but the copter will not let them escape. It appears the military has caught them, but a voice over a loud speaker tells them that everything is okay and to get inside the aircraft. The two hesitate and then enter the copter. We don't learn until later if everything is indeed okay.

Reversals can occur at or near the beginning of a scene. This type of reversal, though, requires a slightly different approach from reversals that come later in the scene.

Let's look at an early-in-the-scene reversal in *Out of Africa*. In the doctor's office, Karen learns that she has syphilis. The remainder of the scene reveals her reaction to what in those days was virtually a death sentence, and ends with her decision to return to Denmark to fight the disease.

Using a reversal to open a scene precludes you from transcribing some initial reaction and then terminating the scene. If you open your scene with a dramatic twist, the rest of the scene must build even more tension as it heads toward a payoff. And the end of the scene will require some decision or climactic event that stems from the opening.

Reversals are so significant that everything in a scene must lead to a reversal, be a reversal, or be the reaction to a reversal. Every part of the scene is planned with the reversal in mind. Every action, all of the exposition and characterization, as well as bridging in and bridging out, should center on the reversal. Anything in the scene not relating to the reversal should be cut. Save it for another scene, another screenplay, or that novel you plan to write someday.

Reversals work in part because they are unpredictable. So even if you have created strong and inventive reversals, they will lose their effectiveness if audiences come to expect them in certain situations or at particular times.

A way around this problem is to occasionally add more than one reversal to a scene. In an entertaining little sleeper film, *Harley Davidson and the Marlboro Man*, a seemingly insignificant one-dollar bet proves almost fatal for our heroes. In *Back To the Future*, Marty's first tour of his hometown in 1955 is hilarious because of the contrasts —

reversals — to his hometown in 1985. And in *A Beautiful Mind*, Alicia discovers that John's secret job for the government exists only in his mind when she sees his office covered from floor to ceiling with nothing but newspaper and magazine clippings, and she learns his so-called secret lab is simply a giant, dusty, empty building.

A terrific double reversal emerges in the film M*A*S*H when the hospital director tries to stop a baby's operation in the Tokyo Army Hospital. Putting the director under with gas is one reversal. But to make sure the director won't cause any trouble when he awakens, Hawkeye and Trapper make him the star of a photo session in one of the best "little houses" in Japan. This makes the scene much stronger and funnier.

In *Erin Brockovich*, Ed hires Erin back, but she isn't satisfied with simply being rehired. She demands a ten-percent raise and benefits before she gives Ed any information about the case she was working on. Ed reluctantly agrees.

In Million Dollar Baby, the tragic events surrounding the fight happen only after Maggie, who could probably knock out her opponent with one more punch, stops fighting practically in mid-punch because the bell rings. Her opponent, unfortunately, has no such restraint.

While adding more reversals per scene can be fun and entertaining, it can also make the story so complex or convoluted that it becomes difficult to follow. First, make certain your reader understands what she's reading and then continue to create the magic.

One commonly asked question is *should a writer know the reversal before writing the scene?* Generally, yes. The writer should also know what's going to happen in the scene and what the main conflict will be. I always encourage my students to provide a simple scene-card outline for their entire script (as we discussed in Chapter 2). It doesn't have to be long or complicated. You can create one for yourself on

3 x 5 or 5 x 7 index cards. Using one card to represent each scene from your script, write on each card:

1. The scene number. If you choose to write your scenes out of order, make an educated guess.

2. How many pages the scene will require. Again, make an educated guess.

3. What happens in the scene? Describe it in one or two lines.

4. What is the conflict in the scene? Describe it in one or two lines.

5. The reversal. Describe it in one or two lines.

Your journey through the scene will become easier once you establish these elements. Of course, this in no way excludes the probability that your characters will journey to unexpected places or arrive in unanticipated situations. I always tell my class that if your finished screenplay replicates your outline, then you have encountered one of two conditions:

The first is that you have experienced that rare and glorious providence when the Muses have smiled upon you and you have written an extraordinary script. The second is that you've held back, stuck too close to the genre formula, or felt like you couldn't veer from the original outline. Nine-hundred-ninety-nine times out of a thousand, hope for the first, bet on the second.

If your script changes so much during the writing process, why write an outline at all? Why know your conflicts and reversals beforehand? Because when you get lost, your scene outline will put you back on track. You can more easily determine what each character wants to accomplish by first indicating the conflict that will occur in a scene.

By specifying the reversal, you help ensure that the action in the scene will flow toward the reversal and that there will be a believable reaction to the reversal at the scene's end. Primarily, though, a scene outline is a starting point.

Most writers I know or have worked with need a framework with which to begin their script. Knowing the skeleton of a scene — especially the reversal — clues the writer in as to where he is and how far he must go. Briefly outlining your scenes beforehand will help you stay focused on the big picture even though some of the individual elements of your scenes may change.

I do not believe there is a way to overstate the significance of writing at least one reversal per scene. A reversal, no matter how extraordinary, will not ensure a great scene. But a scene without a reversal is almost certain to fail. A reversal is the glue that binds the scene together. It is the point of emotional change, the surprise, and the main factor that will keep your screenplays alive and well and selling in Hollywood.

There are millions of classic and clever scene reversals. One of the most famous is in *Casablanca* when Rick shoots Major Strasser and doesn't know whether Louie will tell the police. Finally, Louie commands the police to "round up the usual suspects."

Another good reversal occurs in *Shakespeare In Love*, when Henslowe's Rose Theatre is closed because he allowed a woman to rehearse for a production. It appears that *Romeo And Juliet* will not be produced until Burbage, Henslowe's rival, agrees to stage Shakespeare's new play at his theatre, The Curtain.

Here are some other good reversals:

Butch Cassidy and The Sundance Kid: Harvey Logan challenges Butch to a knife fight. But Butch says they first have to get the rules straight.

Harvey hesitates a moment to question the idea of rules in a knife fight. The moment he hesitates, Butch delivers a swift, hard kick to Harvey's crotch.

Chinatown: Detective Jake Gittes is close to discovering what is happening to Los Angeles' water supply when he's captured by several men. To show Jake what happens to "nosy people," the man with a knife slices Jake's nose.

Dave: Dave and Ellen pretend to be President and First Lady look-alikes — and sing a bad rendition of the song, *Tomorrow*, to avoid being identified as the actual President and First Lady.

Them: State troopers discover a little girl who is the lone survivor of a bizarre massacre. She is the one person who can help explain what happened, but all she utters is "Them."

Enigma: British authorities are searching for Tom and Hester, who have taken the enigma machine. They are captured in a barn, but even a thorough search by the police doesn't turn up the machine. When Tom and Hester return home, they pull the enigma machine from a compartment below their car's top-down roof.

Erin Brockovich: Erin offers a glass of water to the opposing council and tells her that it's water from the nearby utility company — the same water the lawyer claims is absolutely safe. The opposing council does not drink the water.

The Aviator: Howard Hughes has been in isolation — barely sane and functioning — shortly before testifying at a hearing in front of Senator Brewster's subcommittee. Everyone expects him to fail, but he's brilliant and shows up Brewster, effectively giving his airline a new lease on life.

Chapter 5
Format and Everyone Else

Format is more than simply a recipe for where everything goes on the page.

"Format is seventy-five to eighty percent of the battle." announced our screenwriting professor during my first class at USC. It sounded ludicrous. After all, other forms of written storytelling focus on content. Sure, spelling, grammar, and punctuation must be correct. But beyond that, writing skill and narrative determine whether a work succeeds or fails.

I quickly learned that my professor was right. Readers often will not even look at a script that's formatted incorrectly. Agents and producers are adamant that a screenplay look professional. After reading and critiquing thousands of scripts myself, I realized that demanding that a screenplay be correctly formatted makes a lot of sense.

Since the next two chapters are about the correct way to put the ink on the paper — or formatting — my editor correctly surmised that it would help readers to see a well-formatted (not to mention a well-written) script to have a visual of how this looks when expertly done.

I didn't want to include an entire screenplay, but as short scripts are becoming quite popular — at least in the contest world — I have placed in the Appendix a copy of *True Magic*, written by Barbara Jacksha, one of my former students. Barbara won the Southwest Writers Screenwriting Contest for her feature length script *Lac Mirage*, and she also has been a semi-finalist in the Gimme Credit Screenplay Competition, a runner up in the Upstart Short Script Competition and the New Mexico Governor's Cup Screenwriting Competition, and an alternate in the Duke City Shootout Script Competition.

With her permission and with my thanks, we offer her script, *True Magic* as an excellent model for good format, writing, and storytelling.

Usually a better formatted script is a better written script. Most readers know this. They realize that scripts with lots of ink (long paragraphs of dialogue and direction), camera angles, numerous parentheticals, too many or too few pages, or page designs only Salvador Dali could love, are destined for the landfill. Also, readers want a well-formatted page because the format itself provides significant details. I demonstrate this to my classes by assigning them the following exercise:

I ask each student to read a produced script and take one page of that script and write it in *blah blah* form. That is, for each letter in each word on the original page, I ask them to change the letter to either a "b", "l", "a", or "h". So if the part of the script appears as

INT. KITCHEN - DAY

DAN works on the blender. From behind, Charlie looks on. Dan nods, it's fixed.

CHARLIE
Go ahead, make my milk shake!

The student would change it to

BLA. BLAHBLA - BLA

BLA blahb bl bla blahbla. Blah blahbl, Blahbla blahb bl. Bla blah, bl'a blahb.

BLAHBLA
Bl blahb, blah bl blah blahb!

The format stays exactly the same. All of the various parts of the page — slug, directions, dialogue paragraph (all explained in the next chapter) — are placed on the page exactly as they are in the original work. What changes are the words.

When students bring the assignment to class, I ask them to exchange papers and tell me as much as they can about the page they are viewing just from the form they see in front of them. From this form you can see

1. One slug line — a change in the audience's view.

2. One short direction paragraph.

3. In that short paragraph, a word is in caps and probably means a new character is introduced.

4. The third word in the second sentence starts with a cap, so another character is in the scene.

5. The character cue has the same amount of letters as the character who was mentioned in the second sentence of the paragraph.

6. He/She is probably the one talking.

7. There is an emphatic short speech.

8. This part of the page paces fairly quickly.

The point is (and I am sure you're way ahead of me here) that a reader can decipher a tremendous amount of information about a script without having to read any of the words. A reader can tell from just the look of the pages how the script paces, whether the description and dialogue are easy or difficult to wade through, and most importantly, if the script appears professional.

Each of these factors is critical. The truth is that the first assessment of your script will take no more than a minute, if that. The reader will quickly check the length of the script, determine if it is correctly bound, and scan through the pages to see if the format appears correct. If everything checks out, he'll then turn to the title page to make certain it looks professional. In an extremely short period of time, the reader will determine whether your script — that precious work that took months of your blood, sweat, and fears to finish — will be considered worthy of a serious read.

When I began teaching, I searched for a book on formatting that was comprehensive and easy to understand. I never found such a book, so I wrote one.

Formatting Your Screenplay covers format basics. It is used not only by my students but by college film-writing programs and screenwriting professionals. (If you would like to order a copy of *Formatting Your Screenplay*, please email me at rick@20thingsbook.com.) Of course, there are now a host of computer programs that help you format your screenplay. But I always caution students not to depend on these programs without first learning the basics. It would be like using a calculator before knowing how to add, subtract, multiply, or divide. How would you know which numbers to use and under what circumstances? Suppose the calculator broke down or the batteries died? What then?

I have read screenplays where the format was right-justified, or where the left-hand margin was too far to the left (throwing every element in the script too far to the left), or where every page was single spaced from the slug to the directions that followed. When I asked my students why they had committed these errors, they answered that it was the way the format program set it up.

My students are generally praised for their format, and at times, good format is the one factor that helps them sell or option their work. In fact, the first student of mine who sold a screenplay got in the door because of, that's right, format. The producer told this student that he read the script because it was the first screenplay he had seen from outside Hollywood that was correctly formatted. The student ultimately sold two scripts to *Fox*.

Despite the new software and the myriad books and classes offered on screenplay writing, poorly formatted scripts still abound. Don't let yours be one of them. A well-formatted script is the key to opening up that first door in Hollywood.

Obviously, format alone will never sell a screenplay, and just as obviously, some writers manage to sell screenplays that are not correctly formatted or even that well written. However, they are usually insiders, people who are already known and trusted by the Hollywood establishment.

While knowing where to place slugs, directions, and dialogue is vital, format is far more complex than simple page placement. You learned earlier in this chapter that the look of each page plays a key role in how the script is seen, read, and interpreted.

Page presentation becomes part of the overall content of the screenplay. It's a tool writers use to manipulate pace and direct emotional response. Let's say you have an action scene in your script. It might play out better if each line becomes a separate paragraph.

So instead of writing the scene like this:

CHASE

Mike's car speeds ahead of his pursuers. He two-wheels a corner. From an intersection just ahead, two cars emerge, blocking the road. Mike spins his car around, now facing the pursuing cars.

Mike speeds his car toward the pursuing cars. At the last second, he jumps his car onto the sidewalk and careens around his pursuers.

PURSUERS

try a quick turn, but they crash into each other. All they can do now is watch.

Mike's car disappears into the distance.

it could be written this way:

CHASE

Mike's car speeds ahead of his pursuers.

He two-wheels a corner.

From an intersection just ahead, two cars emerge.

They block the road.

Mike spins his car around.

He faces the pursuing cars.

Mike speeds his car toward the pursuing cars.

At the last second, he jumps his car onto the sidewalk.

He careens around the pursuers.

PURSUERS

try a quick turn.

They crash into each other.

All they can do now is watch.

MIKE'S CAR

disappears into the distance.

This staccato look indicates fast-paced action that enhances the excitement conveyed through the actual description.

On the other hand, several long paragraphs give the page a greater ink to white space ratio and a more deliberate pacing. For example:

> From the heavily-wired compartment a figure appears. The figure is small, dark, and confused. It moves gingerly at first, but slowly gains strength. Finally, it rises high enough to be identified as a small simian.
>
> George and Warren smile and reach across the compartment to shake each other's hand. The monkey reaches up to grab onto their hands, and for the moment they fail to notice the animal.
>
> Finally, Warren reaches down carefully to pick up the monkey and hold him. The monkey, still groggy, responds at first to the embrace. But when Warren heads toward the cage, the monkey lets out a yelp and bites Warren on the arm.

One problem with screenplay format is that minor fads come and go, and some writers try to keep up with the trends. For a while the capping of all sound cues was dropped. Today, capping certain sound cues has returned. For a while the period after INT. or EXT. was deleted. Lately, the period after INT. and EXT. has been reinstated. The use of CONTINUED at the top and bottom of certain pages appeared on its way to extinction. However, in the script for *Million Dollar Baby*, it reemerges.

Trying to keep abreast of every change in formatting can drive you crazy. I'm not certain that anyone outside the industry can keep abreast of every which way the whim blows. And those whims can change at any time; change, for instance, just as you are finishing your script. So forget the fads and stick with the basics. Good, fundamental format will produce the desired results.

Because ideas are a dime a hundred (inflation being what it is) professional presentation can be the critical factor that gets your script taken seriously. It seems strange and frustrating that presentation should be considered first, but think of it as being a lot like life. The person should matter first, the exterior trappings later. But if that were true, *Playboy* would have a difficult time staying in business. The first essential for success is to make sure your script is dressed for the dance and ready to boogie.

Chapter 6
Formatting Your Screenplay

Correct format is the first sign of a true professional.

Learning format is like learning how to play chess. The first step is to learn the pieces and then to master how they interact.

Formatting has five basic categories:

Slug Lines or Slugs
Direction
Dialogue
Fades and Cuts
Marginals

Slug Lines

Slug lines (hereafter referred to as slugs) are those always-capped single entries that look like this:

EXT. RESTAURANT - DAY

The slug is used to introduce a scene or shot. As discussed in Chapter 1, a shot is simply the slug and everything that follows until the next slug.

The rules for the slug are

1. Using the old typewriter spacing of ten spaces per inch, most computer programs begin the left hand margin at 1.4, or 1 inch and 4 spaces from the left edge of the paper.

2. Slugs should fit on only one line.

3. When you end a shot, whether with direction, dialogue, or a cut such as CUT TO:, you should triple space to the next slug. (The only exception being the very first slug of your screenplay, which you double space from FADE IN:.)

Most of the computer programs now available double space to the slug. And while some of the software defaults can be changed, if you just follow their default spacing it throws off the one-page-of-script-equals one-minute-of-screen time rule that has been true of scripts since well before the use of these programs. I realized this when a student of mine wrote a 111 page script. When the producer who was interested in that script converted it to one of the more popular computer format programs, it suddenly became a 96 page script. So the question then becomes, is this a 111 minute film or a 96 minute film? It does make a difference.

4. You must double-space to whatever follows a slug.

5. Either direction or dialogue must always follow a slug. Never follow a slug with another slug or a cut.

6. Never leave a slug as the last item on the page. That is, never leave the slug without following it with direction or dialogue.

7. Never have more than eight slugs on a page.

8. Beware of silly slugs unless used for a reason. I have seen INT. ALBERT, or INT. CAN. Unless you are doing a film like *Fantastic Voyage* or *Innerspace*, how are you going to show INT. ALBERT or INT. CAN? I have also seen EXT. TABLE. This may be easier to see, but there is no need (at least until the next slug) to concern ourselves about where that table is — either EXT. or INT.

9. Do not number your slugs. (Numbered slugs appear only in production scripts.)

10. Put all slugs in caps.

11. Do not use camera angles.

Direction

Direction delineates the action and describes characters, settings, and objects. It's the means by which you indicate the visual images you want on the screen. For example:

The cue ball slams off two rails, bumps the five ball into the side pocket and stops behind the eight-ball, putting both balls in a direct line with the corner pocket.

Direction is written in single-spaced, prose paragraphs. The margins for directions are flush left, which means they begin on the same vertical space as the slug line. For the right margin, leave a space of between 1" to 1.25" from the right edge of the paper. Never justify the right margin. No matter what precedes a direction paragraph — a slug, dialogue, or another direction paragraph — always double space to the new direction paragraph.

Direction is written in the present tense, which gives the story a feeling of immediacy, as though it was playing on the screen before the reader. And direction follows the same punctuation and grammar rules as other prose.

One excellent way to make your screenplay more readable is to limit your direction paragraphs to four lines or fewer. This is really easier to do than it may seem. Because a screenplay is not prose per se, paragraphs can be broken at any logical place. If you move from one action to the next, change paragraphs. If you move from a general description to a more specific one, you can break your paragraph at that point. Remember, you may have several direction paragraphs follow each other on the page. By keeping them to four lines or fewer, you create a more pleasant page to view and an easier page to read.

Finally, do not describe camera movement or camera angles in direction. In fact, never show camera movement or angles in a screenplay. After all, these elements are the job of the director and cinematographer, not the writer.

Dialogue

Dialogue tells what is said and by whom. It's always written down the horizontal middle of the page and has three distinct parts: the *character cue*, the *speech*, and the infrequently used *parenthetical* — also known as personal or actor's direction.

Character Cue

Begin dialogue paragraphs with the character cue, or speaker's name, in caps. Do not underline or center the character cue. Start the character cue at 4.1 inches, or 41 spaces, from the left edge of the paper, and no matter what precedes it — a dialogue or direction paragraph — always double space to the character cue.

Never leave the character cue as the last item on the page. If there's not enough space on the page for the character's speech to follow the cue, move the cue to the top of the next page.

Speech

Begin the character's speech on the line beneath the cue and continue to single space throughout the speech. Since the speech must read down the center of the page, set your left margin at 2.8 inches, or twenty-eight spaces, from the left edge of the paper, and set your right margin at 5.6 or 5.8 inches, or fifty-six or fifty-eight spaces, from the left edge of the paper.

Parentheticals

The *parenthetical* or *personal* or *actor's direction*, refers to instructions to the actors. They are enclosed in parentheses and placed directly beneath the character cue, or sometimes within the speech itself. When a parenthetical appears directly below the character cue, place the first parenthesis mark at 3.5 inches, or 35 spaces from the left edge of the paper. The best way to handle parentheticals is to not use them. Actors are paid and paid well to interpret their roles in a script. Regardless of how you see it, an actor will play his role the way he feels is right. Most actors do not appreciate writers telling them how to interpret a part.

FADES and CUTS

Fades and *cuts* are those always-capped instructions that begin, advance, and end a full-length film script. Fades begin and end a script. Cuts perform two functions: They end one segment of your script (shot, scene, or sequence) and signal a transition to the next shot. We'll examine fades first.

FADES

Fades consist of FADE IN: and FADE OUT., period. Each is used only once in a film script. FADE IN: begins your screenplay. FADE OUT. ends your screenplay.

FADE IN:

You write FADE IN: in all caps, followed by a colon (:). Triple space from the title on page one — not the Title Page — and begin

FADE IN: at 1.4 inches, or 14 spaces from the left edge of the page, the same margin as for slugs and directions.
FADE IN: appears in no other place in a full-length film script.

FADE OUT.

FADE OUT. marks the end of the screenplay text. It is written in all caps and followed by a period (.) to denote the end of the screenplay. Double-space from your last direction or dialogue in the script to FADE OUT. FADE OUT. begins at 6.1 inches, or sixty-one spaces from the left edge of the paper, like this:

>   FADE OUT.

This is the only time FADE OUT. is used in a film script.

CUTS:

Cuts are slightly more complicated to use than fades. Cuts are the short, always-capitalized elements of the screenplay that tell a reader that a shot, scene, or sequence is finished and that a new shot, scene, or sequence is imminent. In a screenplay you will use only two types of cuts. The first is CUT TO:, the second is MATCH CUT:

Both cuts are capitalized, and written as two words followed by a colon. Both begin 6.1 inches, or sixty-one spaces, from the left edge of the page. Neither is underlined, and neither should ever be the first line on any page.

CUT TO:

CUT TO: tells the reader that one section is finished and a new one follows. Whether the section ends with direction or dialogue, the writer double spaces to the CUT TO:, then triple spaces to the following slug.

CUT TO: should be used sparingly if at all. After all, if you double space to CUT TO:, then triple space to the slug, you will have five spaces full of *bubkes* (nothing). A lot of those equal several pages of, well. . .more *bubkes*.

To avoid this problem, employ cuts only where there is a major change in time, place, and/or action. These changes usually don't take place within a scene. They do occur at the end of some scenes, and at the end of all sequences.

What's a sequence? Glad you asked. A *sequence* is two or more scenes centered on a theme and/or action with a beginning, middle, and end. There are usually no more than six to eight sequences in a film. So if you were to use a CUT TO: at the end of every sequence, your screenplay would probably contain no more than six or seven CUT TO's.

MATCH CUT:

Use MATCH CUT: to bridge shots, scenes, or sequences by focusing on a physical object. For instance:

EXT. PARK - DAY

A man sits on the park bench staring at the headline in the paper.

HEADLINE

MURDERER STILL AT LARGE

                                                                                MATCH CUT:

HEADLINE

MURDERER STILL AT LARGE

INT. NEWSPAPER/EDITOR'S OFFICE - NIGHT

The editor stares at the headline, mumbling to himself. He finally looks up and shouts.

                    EDITOR
     Get Sterling! And get him in here quick!

The time, place, people, and action has been changed and bridged by the MATCH CUT:. MATCH CUT: works well if used sparingly, certainly no more than two times in a script.

Marginals

Marginals denote the small but significant items found on the margins of the page. These items include, title, page numbers, *the end*, and *continued*. Since the title and the end are found only once each in the screenplay, let's cover them first.

Title

On page 1 of the script (not the title page), write the screenplay's title six lines down from the top of the page, or about one and one-eighth inches from the top edge of the paper. Center the title, write it in all caps, and place quotation marks on either side. From the title, triple space to FADE IN:. (And from FADE IN: double space to the first slug.)

THE END

Write THE END on the last page of your screenplay. Place THE END six lines below FADE OUT (if you have six lines.) If you do not have six lines, at least try to double space. THE END should be centered, written in all caps, and underlined. They should be the last words in your script.

Pagination

In a script, a page number appears on every page except page one. Begin numbering four lines down from the top edge of the paper, and 7.2 inches (or seventy-two spaces) from the left edge of the paper. Page numbers may be written in one of three ways:

35

35.

-35-

If you choose the third method, place the first hyphen 71 spaces from the left edge of the page.

Any of the three ways is appropriate for feature scripts. The number followed by a period is almost always used in teleplays and sitcom scripts.

CONTINUED:

Though many screenwriters are dropping the use of CONTINUED:, I include it simply to show you how and why it is or was used.

The top of every page, except page one, begins with either CONTINUED: or a slug. A slug shows you have begun a new shot. A CONTINUED: at the top of the page shows that the shot from the previous page is ongoing.

If a slug appears at the top of a page to indicate a new shot, it follows that the bottom of the previous page was the end of another shot. Therefore, the bottom of that page would either end with direction, dialogue, or a cut.

If a CONTINUED: appears at the top of the page instead of a slug, then the bottom of the previous page should also end with a CONTINUED.

USING CONTINUED:

The top-of-the-page CONTINUED: starts at four lines down from the top edge of the paper, at the same vertical spacing from the left edge of the paper as FADE IN:, slugs, and directions. It is written in all caps and followed by a colon.

The bottom-of-the-page CONTINUED begins at the same vertical line as FADE OUT., CUT TO:, or MATCH CUT:. It is enclosed in parentheses; the first parentheses mark begins at 6.1 or 61 spaces from the left edge of the paper:

>   (CONTINUED)

It is double-spaced down from the final direction or dialogue on the page. Never follow a slug with a bottom-of-the-page CONTINUED. If there is no room for intervening direction or dialogue, the slug must be moved to the top of the next page.

I stated earlier that some writers have stopped using CONTINUED altogether. It's a pain to use, and the fact that you are continuing the shot is both self-evident and not particularly relevant to a script. Check with writers, agents, or others you know in the business and make your own decision about using CONTINUED.

These are the basics in brief. Obviously, other factors play a part in the format and look of your screenplay. Among the most important are generic slugs. What do I mean by generic slugs? Most of the slugs in your script will come from your story — the people, places, and objects from your screenplay. Generic slugs, on the other hand, indicate a specific kind of shot or scene in your script. These slugs are

SERIES OF SHOTS
MONTAGE
SPFX

SFX
POV
BACK TO SCENE
WIDER VIEW
SPLIT SCREEN
INTERCUTTING
INT./EXT. or EXT./INT.

SERIES OF SHOTS and MONTAGE can strengthen a script. But make sure you know what each is and how and when to use them correctly.

A SERIES OF SHOTS is much like a scene in that it's centered on a theme and/or action and has a beginning, middle, and end. But a SERIES OF SHOTS differs in that it's a group of short shots that quickly transport a character through a period of time.

A MONTAGE, on the other hand, includes two or more images that blend into and out of each other in order to create a particular emotional effect. Dreams, nightmares, hallucinations, and photographs provide some of the most common subjects for the movie montage.

When you need special effects, you use SPFX.

For special sound effects, you use SFX.

Again, you will need these, only rarely (if at all).

The other generic slugs such as POV (Point Of View), BACK TO SCENE, and WIDER VIEW, as well as SPLIT SCREEN, INTERCUTTING, and INT./EXT. or EXT./INT. can be used as other ways to view the action or move the action forward. These slugs, which I describe in my first book, should also be employed sparingly.

Abbreviations and Caps

As I mentioned before, there are certain phrases that are always abbreviated and some that are always capped. These include:

MOS - *without sound*. In your screenplay, the direction might be written, "We see two people talking MOS." We see them but cannot hear what they are saying.

AD LIB - General, extemporaneous chatter among a group of people. It is always written in caps.

V.O. - Voice Over. It is used to indicate the voice of someone who can not be physically present in the scene, or the voice of a narrator, reflecting his thoughts, even if he or she is not in the scene. You write it like this:

> TV NEWSMAN (V.O.)
> We have just learned today that
> sales of *20 Things You Must Know
> to Write A Great Screenplay* are going
> through the roof. So if your ceiling
> has a strange hole in it....

If used in dialogue, it is placed on the character cue line, all in caps, with a period after each letter, and enclosed in parentheses. If you use Voice Over in directions, write a lower case (v) followed by a period and a lower case o also followed by a period: v.o.

O.S. - *Off Screen*. It is used to indicate someone who could be physically in or part of the scene, but you have chosen that the audience not see that person at that moment.

> BIG BAD BILL (O.S.)
> Give it up Cody, I'm coming in to get ya.

If used in dialogue, it is also placed on the character cue line, all in caps, a period after each letter, and enclosed in parentheses. If you use Off Screen in direction, write in lower case o.s. If it begins a sentence, the O is capped.

B.g. and F.g. - *background* and *foreground*. They are always abbreviated b.g. and f.g. in directions. If either begins a sentence, the first letter is capitalized. Each letter is always followed by a period.

Other Capitalization Rules

1. Book and song titles should be all capped.

2. As discussed, sounds are capped if they are not a result of the actions of a person or event on screen.

3. Special signs such as SALLY FILE — DETECTIVE painted on a door should be all in caps.

4. When a character is first introduced in the directions of a script, you should put his or her complete name in caps. From then on, the character's name will be written with the usual upper case-lower case rules.

5. The last items that should concern you — but the first that will concern an agent or producer — are your title page and binding.

On the TITLE Page:

1. Begin the screenplay title approximately four inches or 17 lines from the top edge of the paper.

2. Center the title.

3. Write the title in all caps.

4. Enclose the title in quotation marks.

5. Staying centered, triple-space from the title and write the words Written by. The W is in upper case, the rest is in lower case.

7. While remaining centered on the page, double space and write the names of the author or authors. Partners should use an ampersand (&) between their two names.

8. Approximately three-fourths of the way down the page from the top edge, write your contact information in a single-spaced paragraph on either the left or right side. Include a company name (if applicable) and your address, city, state, zip, the telephone number where you can be most easily reached, and your E-mail address.

9. There is disagreement about whether to place the copyright and/or WGA notice on the title page. Some say it's more professional to do so; others say the opposite. This small debate does seem to go about fifty-fifty. So ultimately, it's your call. If in doubt, ask those to whom you are sending the script, or others in the field, if it is okay to do so.

10. Make sure all your pages are numbered consecutively.

For Binding

1. The script should have front and back covers of 110 pound, 8 X 11 inch card stock. Keep front and back covers the same color, and use any color but white.

2. The script, title page, and covers should all be standard three-hole punched.

3. Use two number 6 or 7 brass round-headed fasteners, and fasten them in the top and bottom holes. Flatten out the ends of the fasteners against the back cover.

4. Unless instructed otherwise by an agency or contest, do not put any writing or anything else on either cover or on the side of the script.

This chapter is only a brief survey of formatting. I realize formatting isn't the most exciting or sexiest part of learning how to write a script. It takes hard work to measure page placement and remember lines and spaces. But you are to be congratulated for wading through this section of the book and learning about formatting.

To learn even more about screenplay format or to have a comprehensive reference on format, I suggest buying a copy of *Formatting Your Screenplay*. Remember, the bottom line for any new screenwriter is to first submit a script that looks professional, and a professional looking script is always correctly formatted. Good format then, is critical if you want to advance your script from, "I'm sorry, but this script does not fit our present needs," to, "We're thrilled to inform you. . . ."

Chapter 7
The Good, the Bad, and the Blind Date

Knowing how to pick your protagonist and antagonist makes a dramatic difference in how you develop your screenplay.

Who is the protagonist in *Back to the Future*? Who is the antagonist? Don't answer too quickly!

Okay, the answers are

Protagonist - George McFly (the father)
Antagonist - Marty McFly (the son)

What? That's not what you learned in those college literature classes. Of course not, because those classes taught you about the *literary* protagonist and antagonist. What I am discussing is how to define and use the *dramatic* protagonist and antagonist.

So please suspend your disbelief, arguments, and objections. . .at least until you finish this chapter. I hope by then I will have convinced you that there is a huge difference between the literary and dramatic protagonist and antagonist.

Think for a moment about change. Everyone seeks to improve in some way. Children want to grow up. Adults want to be wiser, richer, more skilled, or more powerful. You want to learn to write screenplays or write better screenplays. But in order to improve, you must change. And change can be an uneasy prospect.

One of the ways we learn to prepare for change is by studying how others cope with change in their own lives, and our stories and epics and tales are a way of doing just that. A large part of what compels us to commit to someone else's story in film is when we experience profound change in at least one of the characters.

This does not necessarily mean that only one person in your screenplay will change. But if you expect someone to buy your script, there must be at least one character who undergoes not just change, but the most critical, momentous, life-altering transformation she will ever experience. That person is your *dramatic protagonist*.

Put simply, the dramatic protagonist is the character who changes the most. Obviously, if a character is living one second and dead the next, she has changed drastically. But you must consider a vast array of changes — emotional, political, social, spiritual — when you create your protagonist. Physical, material, and environmental changes and even shifts in lifestyle, habits, or relationships also should be part of the mix. Consider the entire range of human attributes before deciding which of your characters will undergo the greatest change.

When outlining or writing your screenplay, the place to begin — the anchor for the whole work — is with the protagonist. The protagonist has a goal or a dream she longs to turn into reality. And sometimes that goal is not necessarily a positive one. (In *Ordinary People*, for instance, Conrad wants to commit suicide.) No matter what the goal, the audience will be disappointed if your protagonist attains it without much struggle or opposition, because who the heck wants to pay to see a film without conflict or reversals? Overnight success and ever-after happiness do not make for great cinema.

To repeat, if you allow your protagonist to reach her goal without much effort or opposition, then your screenplay will not translate into compelling drama. Fortunately, there is another character inhabiting your screenplay who will ensure that your protagonist's journey proves challenging. That person is the *dramatic antagonist*.

Let's say the protagonist is on a bicycle (P) and beginning to peddle toward his goal (X).

```
        X
        ^
        ^
        ^
        ^
        ^
        P
```

Now imagine the antagonist on a small, motorized vehicle — something like a moped. Why a more powerful machine? Because at the beginning of every story, the dramatic antagonist is always the more powerful character. She may be stronger, faster, more knowledgeable or clever, richer or more self-assured, but she is at the outset of the story, always the more dominant of the two.

Because the protagonist and antagonist have such a profound effect on each other, their bikes are linked by an invisible but unbreakable chain. So while the protagonist peddles from bottom to top, the antagonist motors right to left.

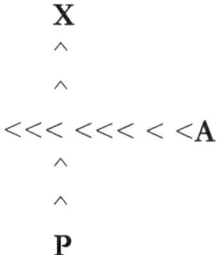

When the stronger character, the antagonist, motors right to left, what happens to the protagonist? Quickly, so quickly it is the first reversal in Scene 1 of the script, the antagonist diverts the protagonist from the original goal, and whether or not the protagonist realizes it, he is headed toward a different objective.

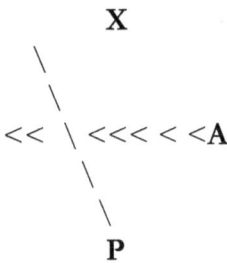

The remaining story centers on how the protagonist either reaches his new goal or is ennobled by his effort. (There is an exception, which I will discuss later in this chapter.) Let's look at some examples:

Forrest Gump - Forrest's goal changes from pleasing his mother to keeping his relationship with Jinny.

Star Wars - Luke's goal changes from attending the academy to destroying the Death Star and the Empire.

Silence of the Lambs - Clarice's goal evolves from simply graduating from the FBI Academy near or at the top of her class to hunting down Buffalo Bill.

Back to the Future - George's goal changes from trying to be invisible to being happy and successful.

Million Dollar Baby - Frankie Dunn's goal changes from managing a male boxer to managing and being a caring surrogate father to a female boxer.

In these films, and just about every other Hollywood film, the change in the protagonist is profound, vital, and familiar.

Familiar? Come on! How many of us have known a serial killer, duked it out in a world championship boxing match, gone back in time, or met a space alien — at least when sober? But I remember an interview I saw with Sylvester Stallone about *Rocky*. Stallone said he couldn't write about an out-of-work actor; that character would be too dull to make the experience exciting, so he wrote about an out-of-work boxer instead. Familiar? You betcha.

Just because the antagonist acts in opposition to the protagonist does not always mean that all antagonists are venal or evil. They can at times be quite benevolent, such as Dr. Berger in *Ordinary People*, Cole Sear in *The Sixth Sense*, or Maggie in *Million Dollar Baby*. While others in the screenplay may (for better or worse) influence the protagonist, when all is said and done, the dramatic antagonist is the one and only character in the story who is most responsible for the change in the protagonist.

These distinctions can be confusing. So let's analyze some film examples to see if we can determine the dramatic protagonist and antagonist. One is the 1977 classic, *Star Wars*; another is *Sideways*, the 2004 Academy Award winner for best script; and the third is the star vehicle, *I Am Sam*.

Who is the protagonist in *Star Wars*? Who changes the most? Who dreams of being a hero but refuses the opportunity when called? The answer must be Luke. But now for the tough question, who is the antagonist?

The answer is not as obvious as it may first appear. Arguments could be made, for instance, for Princess Leia, Ben (Obi Wan) Kenobi, Han Solo, or Darth Vader. Let's take a brief look at each.

At the beginning of the story, Luke's dream is to attend the Academy as his father did before him. But Princess Leia's (or at least her holograph's) call for help motivates Luke to change. But even as he seeks out Obi Wan, Luke is not yet ready to make the journey toward heroism.

Obi Wan becomes both a mentor and father figure to Luke. But still, when Obi Wan asks Luke to join him in an effort to save the princess, he initially refuses.

Han Solo, the mercenary with a heart of gold, challenges Luke's self-image and manhood. But Luke's competition with Han symbolizes not antagonism, but the bonding of friends treading similar paths.

In *Star Wars*, Luke's journey, decisions, adventure, and change all lead back to one character, Darth Vader. After all, Vader pushes Luke from the beginning. Vader is the reason Leia must be rescued, the reason Luke must learn to master the Force, and the reason why he must journey, grow, change, and make a death-defying decision at the second turning point in the story. Luke is certainly influenced by the other characters in the story — some of whom also undergo change — but when the light sabers flare and the star ships battle, it is Darth Vader who forces Luke to change.

In *Sideways*, Miles, the morose Junior High English teacher with a fascination for wine, has two major goals at the beginning of the film: The first is to get his novel published, and the second is to reunite with his ex-wife Vicki. But what is immediately on his mind as the movie opens (besides a hangover) is simply getting away from Southern California for a week-long trip to wine country with his friend Jack.

So how does Miles change? He attempts to start a relationship with Maya. He confesses an unpleasant truth to Maya, though he continues to lie to Jack. He shows some courage — foolish though it might be — to help Jack retrieve his wallet. He goes to Jack's wedding after swearing that he wouldn't, is able to talk civilly with his ex-wife Vicki, and even accepts, without going into a huge tailspin, that she is pregnant with her new husband's child. Finally, Miles is able let Vicki go and tries to repair his relationship with Maya.

Who is the antagonist? For whom does Miles really change? It has to be Maya. While Jack pushes the change, Miles isn't able to break with his past or appreciate the fact he has written a good novel until he dates Maya.

Now let's analyze a film where the main character isn't the protagonist. Who changes the most in *I am Sam*? Who transforms herself from a total yuppie concerned only with career and advancement, who can't appreciate or even understand the importance of family, and who never even slows down enough to enjoy a meal, into a more caring and sensitive individual who tries to make time for family and others? It is Rita Harrison, Sam's lawyer. And for whom does she change? The answer could be Sam or Lucy, but when you analyze the film, it is Sam who enters Rita's life and forces her to rethink her priorities. Even though he is the main character, Sam is the antagonist and Rita is the protagonist.

A debate usually arises when I introduce this example and begins with the statement, 'But the protagonist is the main character.'

In film, the main character is always the hero but not always the protagonist. Why? Because in film, the person who changes the most does not always have to be the main or lead character.

When it comes to populating your screenplay, one of the first decisions you must make is to choose your protagonist and antagonist. In other words, to determine which of your characters will change the most and which of your characters will be most responsible for that change. Once you have designated these two characters, you must realize that one of them will always be your main character or hero.

How do you know which of your characters is your hero? Look at the role each plays in the script. Keep in mind that moviegoers, especially American moviegoers, hold a particular fondness for the character who pushes the action forward. Why do you think those shoe ads say, *Just do it?* Because whether the mover or shaker is a good guy or not, the crowd identifies with the character who executes (all meanings intended). This can be good or somewhat frightening depending on your viewpoint and that of your characters.

Despite the folklore, Bonnie and Clyde weren't just a happy-go-lucky couple seeking a unique means of redistributing wealth. They also killed a few people. But who does the audience cheer for and who are they concerned about? (You get no free popcorn for the obvious answer.) Which characters drive the action in the *Friday the Thirteenth, Halloween,* and *Nightmare on Elm Street* films? Who pursues; who runs? The evil-doers are the characters many in the audience support. I always figured that with the right campaign manager one of these guys could be elected President. After all, they're resolute, have a solution to the population explosion, and know how to get a lot of money from people. In other words, the perfect candidates.

Let's return to the question I posed at the beginning of this chapter: In *Back to the Future*, who is the protagonist and why? Who is the antagonist and why? Who changes the most?

Marty changes some. He becomes more confident in his music, his cleverness, and his ability to make quick, decisive decisions. But who begins the film as a first-class *wuss?* Who has absolutely no confidence in himself, his family, his abilities, or his significance as a human being? And who by the film's end has turned all this around one-hundred-eighty degrees? It is, of course, dear ole' Dad.

Okay, George is the protagonist. But who changes him? True, George must confront Biff, but he first must find the confidence within himself take control of his life. He must — for his own sake and especially for Marty's — ask Lorraine to the dance. Who forces George to reassess his actions, and who clearly embraces the role of the antagonist? (Again, you do not get free Milk Duds for the correct answer.) It is Marty. He's the antagonist.

Why then is Marty the main character? Because he pushes the action for most of the movie, and anytime a character drives the action or plot for half the film or better, that person usually commands main character status.

War Games and *Erin Brockovich* operate in much the same way as *Back to the Future*. In *War Games* David pushes the action both by playing the "Game" and for stopping it. David's influence and persistence turns Dr. Falken (the protagonist) around, and makes him instrumental in helping to save the world. Thus David satisfies not only the role of the antagonist, but also the roles of main character and hero.

In *Erin Brockovich*, though lawyer Ed Masry changes drastically by risking his entire career and future by taking on a lawsuit he never intended to accept, it is Erin who drives the action through almost three quarters of the movie.

In most films, however, the protagonist is the main character.

Conrad in *Ordinary People*
John Book in *Witness*
Dr. Malcolm Crowe in *The Sixth Sense*
Will in *Shakespeare in Love*
John Nash in *A Beautiful Mind*
Roxy in *Chicago*
Frankie in *Million Dollar Baby*

Even when he's not the main character, the antagonist still plays a major role in the story.

In *Ordinary People*, Conrad must first seek help before he can improve. But he responds positively only to Dr. Berger. It is Berger who pushes and prods Conrad. It is Berger who is Conrad's transition agent. And it is Berger who Conrad trusts enough to accept the traumatic truth that allows him to experience a new beginning.

In *Witness*, Rachel probably grows more than most dramatic antagonists. Certainly, she holds to her Amish tradition, but she is also a woman captivated by a forbidden relationship with "the Englishman" and thus qualifies as the ideal candidate responsible for the changes in John Book.

In *The Sixth Sense*, Cole Sear allows Dr. Crowe to help him (Cole) change his life for the better.

In *Shakespeare in Love*, Viola is instrumental not only in creating and shaping *Romeo and Juliet*, but also in forcing Will out of his writers' block and allowing him to find his soulmate.

And in *Million Dollar Baby*, Maggie's heart and work ethic clearly turn Frankie around and permit him to have the kind of father-daughter relationship with her that he missed with his biological daughter, Katy.

There are times when the protagonist fails to reach his goal but is ennobled by his effort. In *Twelve Monkeys*, James Cole fails to stop the release of the virus, but he ennobles himself by discovering who actually released the virus as well as by his efforts to prevent its release. Go back to *Easy Rider*. The America that Billy and Captain America seek literally and figuratively shoots them down. In *Steel Magnolias*, Shelby achieves her dream of motherhood, but it comes at a high price. And in *Million Dollar Baby*, Maggie and Frankie's goal is one punch away but, tragically, so is the devastating reversal. Again, the goal is not actually achieved, but because of the protagonist's actions, nobility is.

In some films the protagonist actually achieves his original objective, but does so in a completely different way from how he imagines it will happen. The screenwriters, Cash and Epps, who wrote the screenplays for such films as *The Secret of My Success* and *Top Gun*, often had their protagonists reach their original goals in very unexpected ways. Let's review *The Secret of My Success* and *Top Gun* as examples.

In *The Secret of My Success*, Brantley expects to work his way up from the mail room and become CEO of the company at some point in the distant future. But after just six months, he has achieved far more than he ever imagined.

In *Top Gun*, Maverick wants to be the top pilot in his class, but what he does achieve comes at the price of losing his best friend, discovering the truth about himself and his father, and leaving the Top Gun school and then returning. Maverick becomes a top pilot in a way he never dreamed he would.

Because the protagonist must change, continuous or serial characters are usually not protagonists. Indiana Jones and James Bond are certainly heroes but not protagonists. They are responsible for the changes in the protagonists — Indy for Marion in *Raiders of the Lost Ark* and James Bond for one of many double-entendre-named women in his numerous films.

While character change may matter less in action-adventure-thriller-type movies, we still need characters we can care about, cheer for, and identify with. Regardless of how cartoonish the story, a clear protagonist and antagonist are not only welcome, but essential.

Okay, so films are not only about how the protagonist achieves his goal, but about how he changes in the process. What are some of the ways we can communicate this change?

Since film is visual, a fundamental way to indicate change in film is by showing it. Modifying dress, mannerisms, speech patterns, or even habits can reflect changes. By endowing your characters with habits or traits at the beginning of the film that you know will change by the end, you will succeed in portraying (through these outward changes) the heart and soul of your characters.

In *Turner and Hooch*, remember how Turner was so fastidious at the beginning of the film and how relaxed he was at the end? That is a brilliant but simple display of change. At the end of *Back to the Future*, George plays tennis, bosses Biff, has his first novel published, and appears to have a most successful life. At the end of *Chinatown*, Jake Gittes has to be dragged away from a situation in which he swore he would never again become involved. And at the end of *Sideways*, Miles risks driving up-state to see Maya when he wouldn't even ask her out earlier in the film.

We will discuss other reasons you must have a clear dramatic protagonist and antagonist in chapters 10 through 13. The most important things to remember for now are that movies are about characters and their interactions, and a good story must center on and be about those who seek to better themselves through a journey of change.

Chapter 8
A Hero is More Than a Sandwich (It's Also More Than a Beefcake)

Know your hero, for the hero will always carry your screenplay.

What is a hero? Who is a hero? Do we need heroes? Heroic myths, legends, and stories have been told by every culture since the first caveman created the first drama. It seems that humans have always identified with the courageous individual who triumphs over great odds in order to help her family, friends, or community.

These many-told tales were handed down by generations of storytellers who had a gift for holding and mesmerizing an audience. Their heroes slayed dragons, explored unknown territories, and fought for truth, justice, and freedom.

Some of the most important writings and theories about the hero are those of Joseph Campbell. Whether you are reviewing *Hero with a Thousand Faces* or tuning in to Bill Moyers' PBS series in which he interviewed Campbell extensively about myth, you realize that the hero's journey, as Campbell labels it, is one of the invariables of storytelling.

By studying Campbell, we recognize the similarity of characters, stories, and themes from every country, in every culture, and during every age, and we come to understand that the stories we tell and the heroes we create come from a human consciousness little changed from two million plus years ago when Leaky's Lucy trekked across the plains of Africa.

In Chapter 7, we learned how to identify the dramatic protagonist, the dramatic antagonist, and the hero. Many screenwriting teachers and books use the term protagonist and hero interchangeably, but the two are not always the same.

The main character of your story may be either the protagonist or the antagonist, but he is always the hero. The hero is the character who pushes the action for more than half the screenplay. He is the character who garners the most screen time, and the one the audience generally identifies with as they progress through the story. Usually, the hero is the protagonist. However, sometimes the hero is the antagonist; for example, Marty in *Back to the Future*, David in *War Games*, and Erin in *Erin Brockovich*.

To clarify which of the two characters — protagonist or antagonist — is the hero, I like to label them as either *protagonist hero* or *antagonist hero*. These labels clearly identify the characters' role in both the hero's journey and in the Hollywood Script Structure.

Yes, the reason the antagonist is the antagonist is because she is most responsible for the change in the protagonist. But there is a difference between the type of story where the protagonist gradually takes control of her life — and of the entire story — by the end of the second act, and the type of story where the antagonist controls the action and story for well over half of the script. Let's look at some examples of antagonist hero films.

In *Back to the Future*, Marty must find a way to unite his future parents — George and Lorraine — and get back to 1985. Marty pulls George through a variation of the hero's journey by prodding George to ask Lorraine to the dance and win her heart. But until George defies Biff three quarters of the way through the film, he is still the side-car on the Harley, the pawn in the chess game, the dummy in the Bridge hand.

In *Erin Brockovich*, Erin stumbles on a pro-bono case that the law firm she works for has put on the back burner. She wants to investigate the case and asks Ed for permission to follow up on it. He grants her request.

Ed has no real idea of the depth or complexity of the case Erin is investigating. But his casual consent is the catalyst that changes his future, his firm's future, Erin's future, and the lives of hundreds of people affected by the utility company the firm is prosecuting.

Erin and Ed build a case against the utility company. There are several scenes involving meetings where Erin's charm, intelligence, and wit save the day. But when Ed holds a meeting of the townspeople to get them to sign on to arbitrating the case, they begin to walk out on him. This time, Erin can't save Ed, but she doesn't need to. Ed gets the townspeople back on his side with an impassioned speech about how the victims of Love Canal are still waiting to get their money many years after their case went to trial.

While Erin is certainly the antagonist hero, it is Ed (the protagonist) who takes the risks, pushes the suit, and ultimately takes charge of the big meeting, his career, and his life.

You might want to study a film such as *Men In Black*, in which Jay is the protagonist but Kay is the hero, and analyze it for yourself. Watch it, or watch it again, and see how it all works out for the hero and the protagonist. See where the journey takes both main characters and how that dynamic enhances the story.

A thorough understanding of Campbell's basic tenets can be an incredible tool to help you better reveal character, exposition, and direction in your screenplay. Also, a knowledge of the hero in the hero's journey — as well as of the hero's journey itself — can help you keep each of your main characters on course and headed toward a resolution that will enable them to better fulfill their roles and destinies in the story.

Chapter 9
Building Character

You and your audience must care about the characters you've created.

Frankly, my dear, someone must give a damn. Audiences need someone to care about or they won't care about the story or the script.

Characters are more than contrivances to carry a plot or deliver a message. Well before FADE IN:, the characters who inhabit our pages should be living, breathing, sentient beings whose cares, dreams, and lives have affinity with an audience. I will be the first to admit that the Hollywood film is a plot-propelled product. But I will also be the first to admit that over my years of writing, teaching, and critiquing, I have learned the benefit of sculpting well-drawn characters.

This statement appears at the very end of *The Last Tycoon*, F. Scott Fitzgerald's unfinished novel about Hollywood:

Action is character.

That is as concise a description of Hollywood film as any. Yet this simple statement fails to answer the most difficult of questions: *How do we screenwriters fashion convincing, compelling, and sustaining individuals within our visual, plot-driven, and performance-oriented discipline?*

There isn't a one-size-fits-all solution. Screenwriters create, destroy, and manipulate characters. It is your right — or blessing some would say — to well. . .to play God. But the characters in your fictional world, like the characters in the real world, also have rights, privileges, responsibilities, and free will. And these human attributes may not always sync with what you want from your characters. Characters are not puppets after all. They are your friends, family, children, enemies, associates, acquaintances, and yes, even you. Ask yourself, *do any of these folks always respond the way I want them to?*

If your characters are real, they must be constructed as such. They have parents. They have history. They have dreams. They possess strengths and weaknesses. Those who teach and write about character creation say that even the most flawless character isn't without flaw, and even the most flawed character has some redeeming value. This places you back at square one. Characters are individuals, and you have to deal with it.

Okay, but how do you deal with it? Before consulting the experts, you need to recognize that all the world is indeed a stage and you need not journey to exotic, far-flung time zones to find the characters who will drive and thrive in your particular work.

One way to begin creating characters is to analyze people. Watch, study, and listen to others. Make observational notes about people you know and see every day. Unlike Harriet in *Harriet the Spy*, who focused her writing on the bad habits of others, or Blanche DuBois in *A Streetcar Named Desire*, who always relied on the kindness of strangers, we should strive for objectivity when appraising the strengths and weaknesses of those we research.

Watching people, absorbing details, and noticing nuances that are otherwise easily missed is a helpful talent. It takes incredible concentration, dedication, and just plain hard work to master those kinds of skills. But there are a few strategies that can help.

First, you do not have to be in (or at least get a word into) every conversation. Many times it's best to listen, watch, and absorb what people say no matter how ridiculous you believe the exchange. You are not going to solve the mystery of who shot JFK at your cocktail party. (Oliver Stone might, but you won't.)

Watch for who says what. Why do people believe the things they say? Do they actually believe them or are they just stirring the pot? Watch how people say things and notice their body language. Notice group dynamics. Who leads? Who is loud, quiet, shy, outspoken, fanatic, etc.? How do groups dissolve? How do groups re-form?

Some people love people-watching. Others love situation-watching. The latter clues us in to the way we respond and interact with each other, but tells us very little about how we view ourselves. Obviously, it's best to balance these two types of examination. Both exercises are necessary to discern the true nature of people and translate it to the screen.

Most books and articles about building characters stress the importance of your character's *inner* as well as outer goals. Both Marty and George McFly, for example, want to develop into more worthy human beings. James Edwards in *Men In Black* needs to find an authority figure he can truly respect. And Erin Brockovich needs to have people around her who respect and honor who she is and what she does.

Another way to understand others is to experience that which is unique in our own surroundings. To thine own self be *new*. Seek out different people, places, and events. Participate and watch. Play and be a fan. Read, see, write, notice.

In Julia Cameron's wonderful book, *The Artist's Way*, she suggests setting aside one day each week for a special outing. Plan to go to a place or event you haven't been to before or haven't been to in a long time. Visit a museum, a planetarium, or attend a lecture.

An intriguing experiment on the subject of finding the new in the familiar was implemented before a Super Bowl. A therapist found eighteen people who didn't care that much about football. She asked them to watch the entire game and notice special, new things they had not seen before. The people in the experiment who noticed more new things came away appreciating the game more than the others, those who noticed the most new things actually enjoyed the experience, and a few even became fans.

The obvious point — which I will make nevertheless — is that if you concentrate on the present moment and seek out the unique, the unfamiliar and previously unseen, you may learn to appreciate what has been there all along. And who knows, those things you missed before but caught now may one day bring about a rewarding return.

There are added benefits to always seeking out the new. The first is that the familiar doesn't get old; you'll see normal, everyday things with new eyes and new insight. The second is that when something really new — such as moving to a new city or state — does manifest itself, you will be more prepared for it. And the third is that you never know what wonders you might discover that may enrich your life.

What does all this have to do with creating characters? How you perceive the world has much to do with who you are. To view and render objective assessments of human behavior takes a great deal of wisdom, awareness, and experience. The more you have, the more your characters will have. And the more you know about your characters, the better you will be able to communicate that knowledge each time your characters appear in your script.

Entire books and any number of magazine articles have been written on character development. There are good writers and teachers (sometimes one and the same) who can supply valuable insight into the process of creating real characters for your plot and story.

Richard Walter's book, *Screenwriting*, contains good, solid principles on the theory of character portrayal. His suggestions on how to add depth to your characters and even appeal to your villains are excellent.

I have read and used the three chapters on characterization in Syd Field's *Screenplay* more times than I care to count; they are good starting points for character development in your own script.

John Sayles' *Thinking in Pictures* is the best book I have read on the entire process of movie making. His approach to one of my favorite films, *Matewan*, is a lesson in integrating characters into all other facets of film.

Several computer programs have been developed that help with character development. Most of them ask questions about your character or provide a checklist to make certain you have covered as many character attributes as possible.

Of course, it is possible to save the several hundred dollars these programs cost and create your own checklist and questionnaire. Or you can use the one I provide at the end of this chapter. This is not the definitive checklist or personality review. I include it because it has been helpful to others, and I hope it will be for you.

IN THE BEGINNING

A. To make a character a real, live, believable, sentient human being, start with a checklist.

CHECKLIST

I Character Details

A. Sex
B. Age
C. Height
D. Weight
E. Race
F. Eyes

G. Hair
H. Skin

II Appearance

A. Clothes
B. Posture
C. Movement
D. Speech
E. Any unusual or identifying mark(s)

III Back Story

A. Birthday (Time and Place)
B. Name
C. Parents or guardians
D. Home life
E. Parent's life style
F. Parent's educational level
G. Parent's occupations
H. Parent's financial situation
I. Siblings
J. Education of children — especially the main character
K. Religious training and/or education
L. Parent's politics
M. Parent's values

IV Present (Main character)

A. Age
B. Education
C. Occupation
D. Income
E. Assets
F. Social position

G. Political beliefs and commitment
H. Religious beliefs and commitment
I. Sexual orientation
J. Marital status
K. Relationship with
   Parents
   Siblings
   Lovers
   Spouse and/or exes
   Own children
   Friends
   Co-workers
L. Lifestyle
M. Character's goals for his or her children
N. Recreation

V Motivations

A. Outlook on life
B. Outlook on self
C. Most important goals
D. Most important values
E. Temptations
F. Strengths

VI What are the character's

A. Turn-offs
B. Fears
C. Frustrations
D. Vices
E. Disappointments
F. Failures
G. Turn-ons
H. Goals

I. Skills
J. Delights
K. Successes

VII Write at least one more page about your character. Discuss everything you left out in the above description.

This checklist is for your benefit. Remember, the more you know about your characters, the easier it will be to portray them in your story.

Now, like Frankenstein's monster, you have put the parts together, but you still need the electricity to make him live. How do you do that? I have no easy answers, but I do have some suggestions.

1. Study people. Take notes, make commentary, and write descriptions about people.

2. Create a character from a combination of people you know. Don't get too close to any one person, though; court houses are not pleasant places to renew acquaintances with old friends.

3. Interview your character. Become your character and answer questions from his perspective. What transpires, what is discovered, and what new insights are uncovered might surprise you.

4. Intriguing characters have traits that go against the grain. A stock car driver, for instance, might enjoy listening to grand opera (instead of the Grand Ole Opry) while she works on her car.

5. Good characters have goals. Make certain your character wants to accomplish something.

6. Give your character, especially the protagonist, traits at the beginning of your script that you know will change by the end.

7. Even an evil character needs to have something sympathetic or likable about him. Also, give your evil characters a goal and a reason for that goal.

8. Benevolent characters have flaws and weaknesses. Make certain you include these when creating your good guys and gals.

9. Talk to working actors and ask them what they think makes a character memorable.

10. Go to movies and analyze the characters. Do the main characters seem real to you?

11. Do not create a character specifically for a particular actor or actress. If that person is not available, your film script could be dead. Along those same lines, never write such a detailed description of a character that it limits the number of actors or actresses capable of playing the role.

12. While physical attributes such as hair color, eyes, etc. should be in your checklist, they should be mentioned in your script only if they are vital to the plot.

13. Make sure your character is unique and not derivative of a character you have seen on TV or in a movie.

14. If you know how to make astrological charts that include the planetary alignments, houses, etc., you may want to use them. Many writers use astrology to create terrific characters.

15. Make your characters flexible enough to adapt and respond believably to the situations in your story.

16. Discover what else you can write, do, and experience to make your characters come alive.

Hollywood film is driven primarily by plot. But you must do everything possible to make your characters as exciting, engaging, and real as your story. Take the time and effort to define and develop the most realistic and engaging characters possible. And make certain that your audience has characters to root for and believe in. Because regardless of how clever, exciting, or splendid your plot, it won't amount to much without terrific characters.

Chapter 10
Acting Out

The three-act structure is the basis for every screenplay.

Three thousand years ago in his quintessential study of drama, Aristotle wrote in *The Poetics* that the structure of drama has a beginning, middle, and end.

Great, you think. Some guy stays famous for 3000 years because he figured out a plot has a beginning, middle, and end. I'm surprised some sportscaster isn't famous for first articulating that every baseball game has a winner and a loser.

Actually, Aristotle was the first writer to set down rules for drama. And it is these rules, tightened and modified, that form the backbone of the kind of scripts we write today.

Three-Act Structure:

The beginning, middle, and end of a script are the three separate, distinct parts we call acts. In a feature-length film, this three-act structure usually contains between 100 and 120 pages. That is, if each 8" X 11" page of your script represents approximately one minute of actual screen time then 120 of these one-minute pages should equal a two hour movie.

Each act in the three-act structure has a name and a classification. They go by a host of *nom de plumes*:

Act I, Act II, Act III
Beginning, Middle, and *End*
Introduction, Problems, Resolution
Involve, Evolve, and *Resolve*

There is a mathematical balance among the three acts. And there are specific requirements and functions for each act, which I will discuss later. All of these elements are a vital part of the Hollywood Script Structure, and closely examining this portion of the structure is essential for crafting a cohesive and compelling script.

The Three Acts

The first act covers approximately one-quarter of your script. It can end, in some instances, as early as page 25 or as late as beyond page 30. The standard length, however, is in the 25-30 page range.

Act II is the middle half of your screenplay. It commences immediately after Act I and ends somewhere in the 75 to 90 page range — usually in the 80s. Act II is not only the longest section of a screenplay, it is often the most difficult to write. Partially because of its length, this middle section is where most writers need to be vigilant in order to maintain their focus, freshness, and force.

The last act is the final one-fourth of your script. Too many times third acts portray nothing more than *SLAM-BAM, I'm quite a man* action sequences. They are Chanukah, Christmas, Kwanzaa, New Years, and Super Bowl Sunday all rolled into one. Final acts can be as short as fifteen minutes (pages) or as long as 30 — though they are usually somewhere in between.

Now that we have identified the mathematical balance, let's examine content.

Act I - Introduction

Before anything can be accomplished in a film, all of the major elements pertaining to the film must be presented. The major characters must be introduced. *Time* and *place* must be specified. The *tone* and *pacing* of the script should be clear. *Genre* must be apparent. That is, we need to know quickly if the script is a mystery, western, action-adventure, comedy, parody, drama, or other genre. The writer should also hint at the themes of the film and make the story line evident by the middle of the act.

Finally, the first act is usually the place to begin at least one of your subplots — those secondary stories that add depth and dimension to your script. Subplots crisscross the main plot line to help or hinder the protagonist in her effort to reach her goal. We will discuss subplots further in Chapter 16.

A Sundance Film Festival winner for best script and picture, *You Can Count On Me*, introduces all of the major script elements at a slow but steady pace. The opening tragedy illustrates Sammy's (Samantha) and her brother Terry's plight. The movie's themes of death, family, religion, law enforcement, culture clash (small town values versus corporate climate), sex, love, and relationships are revealed in various ways in Act I.

All the major characters in the movie are introduced as well. Sammy's strained relationship with her brother Terry becomes apparent in the first act, as do her other relationships — with her ex, her boss, her boyfriend, and her son, Rudy Jr. The first act introduces all these story elements. How Sammy comes to terms with them constitutes the main story line for the entire script.

Act II - Problems

The transition into Act II (detailed in the next chapter) is one of the most vital points in the entire script; it is the point where the protagonist is put into an unfamiliar situation and must respond in a novel way in order to survive.

The second act is what I call the problem act. Once you decide on your protagonist (the character who changes the most) you must now overwhelm her with countless problems.

A blanket statement such as *the more problems the merrier* is not completely accurate. There can be situations where the protagonist is so overwhelmed the audience will never believe in her deliverance. Some have complained that even *Chinatown* (which I consider more or less sacred) is so convoluted by the time Act III arrives that it makes *Buckaroo Banzai* appear realistic by comparison.

I, obviously, disagree. But what makes movies fun is that audiences get to decide these things for themselves.

The best way to satisfy the criteria for Act II is to inundate the protagonist with constant and increasingly more difficult problems. Your protagonist may be able to overcome many of these challenges during the second act, but the degree of difficultly must increase dramatically as the resolution draws nearer.

The problems the protagonist encounters must be greater than she has ever faced before, challenge her on every level, and force her to reach deep inside to reveal strength, perception, and cunning not previously displayed — though perhaps suspected.

My favorite metaphor for a second act comes from the Chuck Norris film, *Lone Wolf McQuade*. McQuade's truck, with McQuade unconscious inside, has been pushed into a man-made pit. The bad guys bury the truck under the landfill of dirt and gravel and commence a premature victory celebration. But from under the burial chamber comes a rushing, blasting RUMBLE. Seconds later the truck roars from the pit. Dirt and rocks fly, smoke gushes, and Lone Wolf is on his enemies like *Entertainment Tonight* on a Michael Jackson rumor.

Second acts are no different. Bury your protagonist under a pile of problems. Leave her trapped without much air or space and fighting overwhelming odds, and then let her find a way to extricate herself from that unbelievable predicament.

The middle act must tempt, challenge, assault, and threaten your protagonist. It must force him to quickly adapt to the new world of danger, strife, and strangely enough, opportunity, that you have created for him. Act II affirms that deep in the recesses of the protagonist's soul there exists the spirit and courage needed to see the adventure through regardless of the outcome. In essence, it assures the audience that the correct protagonist has been chosen for this challenging journey. Second acts also add new subplots and continue developing the subplot(s) from Act I.

Sammy's problems proliferate in Act II of *You Can Count On Me*. While Sammy has undertaken the responsibility of keeping a house and raising a son, Terry has been a vagabond. This keeps an emotional distance between Sammy and her brother, a distance Sammy hates but which seems to strengthen each day Terry is there. What makes Sammy even more uneasy is the closeness that develops between Terry and Rudy Jr. This subplot tests Sammy when Terry takes Rudy Jr. to meet his father, a man who wants nothing to do with his own child.

Sammy has a comfortable job working at a small-town bank, but a second problem arises when her new boss' corporate attitude and rules threaten to undermine the pleasant and easy-going atmosphere she has established at her workplace. The situation is further complicated when Sammy has an affair with this man.

Finally, Sammy has been dating another man who wants to marry her. She's not happy in this relationship but leads him on anyway because she's afraid of being completely alone.

The challenges Sammy faces in trying to preserve her family and find her moral compass make for a compelling second act.

Act III - Resolution

The transition to Act III is one of the most important points in your screenplay. Because of this specific transition, the third act always belongs to the protagonist, and it is up to her to make the most of it.

In Act III (the resolution act) your protagonist will either reach her goal or be ennobled by her effort. In Act III, we find the protagonist struggling through the most difficult time of her life. Whatever problems she has faced or overcome in the past will seem like a day on *Sesame Street* compared to what is about to happen.

Incidentally, this final plight occurs in all genres — including romance and romantic comedy. In the romance genre, the struggle is about whether two people will become a couple by the end of the film. Their non-coupling would be, presumably, a psychological blow meaning death of spirit, a fulfilling future, and ultimate happiness.

Whatever the struggle, this swiftly approaching confrontation doesn't appear without warning nor does it strike an unprepared protagonist. Each challenge the protagonist faced earlier in the story has been practice for the climatic engagement. But it is during Act III that the true stakes are revealed, and where catastrophe or triumph await at every turn.

In Act III of *You Can Count On Me*, Sammy asks her brother to leave, ends her affair, and expresses her true feelings to the man she's dating. At work, Sammy stands up to her boss and establishes a more honest relationship with her son.

Once Terry has left, we get a brief glimpse of Sammy driving back through town — the same glimpse we saw of her at the beginning of the film. The brief ending reinforces the idea that while things may appear outwardly the same, our protagonist has undergone an internal metamorphoses. Sammy still has questions and problems she must deal with, but she is now ready to address them in a stronger and more effective fashion than she was able to at the beginning of the story.

To reinforce how the three-act structure works, let's study three other films, *War Games*, *Men in Black*, and *Million Dollar Baby*.

The question debated in the first thirteen minutes of *War Games* (almost half the first act) is will a soldier in the military chain of command that controls our nuclear missiles defy orders and refuse to push the button that will trigger World War III?

The visual presentation of this dilemma makes for an exciting opening, but on first examination it seems to have little to do with the plot. Actually, it has everything to do with the plot. Because of one soldier's reluctance to turn the key during the test run — which as far as he knew, would have instigated World War III — the military decides to entrust its entire operating system to a computer program that will follow all orders without sentiment or regret, a decision that will prove fateful soon afterwards.

David, our hero, is introduced in the first act. His modern day Goliath — the computer program installed by the military — is already in place. And by the end of the first act, David has interacted with his Goliath in a way that will ultimately have terrifying consequences.

By the end of Act 1 the genre is unmistakable, the situation, direction, and style have been clearly defined, and the major characters — David, his girlfriend, the military brass, and Dr. Falken — have been introduced.

Hold it! Dr. Falken? But he wasn't even mentioned in the first act.

One reminder: We learned in Chapter 3 that a character does not have to be physically present in a film to be introduced. A character is on screen when he's discussed by the other characters in the film, a representative of that character appears on screen, or his physical presence is seen, even if that presence is on a film or tape.

Dr. Falken appears many times in the first act of *War Games*. How? Falken created the very computer program upon which the military now completely relies. David shows a film Dr. Falken made of himself and his family. We also learn a lot more about Dr. Falken when David tries to break his code so he can play the games on his computer screen.

David breaks the code at the end of Act I, and is now able to play games such as Falken's Maze, tic-tac-toe, chess, and the one he feels he must try, GLOBAL THERMONUCLEAR WAR.

So the computer program is Falken. The game selection is Falken. Falken's Maze is Falken. The information that helps David break into the system comes from finding out about Falken. Thus, Dr. Falken has a larger role than David in the first act of the movie even though he is never physically present.

Dr. Falken again has a larger role than David in the second act even though he is physically present only near the end. Of course, David is still our hero, but it is Dr. Falken who ultimately must decide between annihilation or atonement. David's problems may have engulfed him, but there is no way for him to win without Falken. David can beg, plead, or demand, but without Falken's epiphany he cannot save himself or the world.

In *War Games*, each moment of the action determines the fate of the human race. Falken must get himself and David inside NORAD before the doors close off their last hope. Once inside, Falken must persuade the military that what appears on the computer screen is only a simulation, and that the correct response is no response. Falken succeeds. There is great relief until Joshua, the GLOBAL THERMONUCLEAR WAR game, demands that the game be completed.

Falken must then make a crucial decision on how to stop the real GLOBAL THERMONUCLEAR WAR game from being played. For those of you who have not seen *War Games*, I leave the spectacular ending for you to experience.

Falken completes his personal metamorphosis in the second act and helps David exercise his power and intelligence to try to save humankind. The resolution and ending visually and verbally assure the reader and audience that the change in Falken is permanent.

The opening of *Men in Black* follows a four-winged insect as it soars precariously close to zooming traffic and then darts up to sail across the image of the full moon — reminding us somewhat of the shot from E.T. where the boys' bicycles fly across the image of the full setting sun. Ultimately, the insect smashes against the window of a van driving too fast on a back-country road.

Already tone and genre have been established. The comedic tone is obvious and the main alien bad guy (or bug) has been implied. Kay and the secret alien-monitoring organization, *Men In Black*, are presented in the next section of the film.

Within the next three scenes, we are introduced to

James Edwards (Jay) as he runs down a cephlapoid.

Laurel Weaver, Deputy Medical Examiner, who is at the police station to tell James about her extraordinary discovery.

Edgar the Bug in human clothing.

By the end of Act I all of the major characters have been introduced, the threat of an alien war that could literally destroy Earth has taken shape, and the main story line begins to hurtle forward.

Problems proliferate in Act II. Why are so many aliens trying to leave planet Earth? What is the meaning of the phrase, "The Galaxy is on Orion's belt?" Where is Edgar the Bug, and with all the land-based interstellar vehicles gone, how will he leave the planet?

Act III is about resolution and ending. The resolution revolves around the actions the Men In Black take to stop Edgar and retrieve the Galaxy. The ending reveals a permanent change in the protagonist.

What about *Million Dollar Baby*? It opens with a prize fight. Frankie Dunn, our protagonist hero, is patching up his fighter, Big Willie, between rounds and yelling instructions at him at the same time. Anyone not clear about the tone and genre of this film needs to spend more time in *Story 101*.

Immediately after the fight, Maggie Fitzgerald approaches Frankie and asks him to train her. He tells Maggie that he doesn't train girls.

Maggie pays hefty fees in advance so she can work out at Frankie's gym. Frankie doesn't want her there, but he can't afford to turn down six months worth of payment. The plot line gels at this point and the story of the relationship between Frankie and Maggie and their quest for a boxing championship begins.

At the end of Act I, Big Willie leaves Frankie for another manager who can get him a quicker championship bout. So what are the problems in Act II?

Frankie agrees to help Maggie, but he still wants her to find another manager.

Maggie finds another manager, but Frankie sees she's not being managed correctly, and during the middle of a fight he steps in to help Maggie win. At this point, Maggie asks Frankie if he's going to leave her again. He tells her, "Never," and their destiny is sealed.

Maggie wins her fights too easily (knocking her opponents out in the first round) and Frankie must resort to paying other managers so their boxers will fight Maggie.

Finally, Frankie has to move Maggie up in classification. He doesn't know how she will do against much tougher opponents.

Even though Maggie cares deeply about her family and tries to care for them, they continue to treat her like dirt.

Maggie is winning the championship fight, but an illegal punch after the bell knocks her down across the ringside stool and she is critically injured.

The last act centers on Maggie's rehabilitation, her realization about her family, and her relationship with Frankie. It's a heart-wrenching testament to the meaning of courage, love, and life itself.

Today's movie scripts certainly rely on ancient techniques. But understanding how the modern three-act structure works is also important. By using the solid principals of the past and combining them with the highly structured form of the present, you will make your screenplay into a producible and marketable product that will be appreciated by filmmakers and audiences alike.

To summarize the three-act structure:

A. There are three acts in every script.

1. Each act takes a specific unit of time — or pages.
2. Each act is separate and distinct.
3. The three acts together make a complete screenplay.
4. The three-act structure is based on artistic considerations, not commercial breaks, as in television.

B. Act length is important. With very few exceptions

1. The first act is approximately the first quarter of the script, regardless of the length of the screenplay.
2. The second act is approximately the middle half of the script, regardless of the length of the screenplay.
3. The third act is approximately the last quarter of the script, regardless of the length of the script.

II. Screenplay Functions

A. The first act is the introductory act.

1. All major characters are introduced.

2. Plot, genre, tone, and direction are introduced.

B. The second act is the problem act.

1. Heap continuous and challenging problems on the protagonist..

2. The problems must be greater than the protagonist has faced before.

C. The third act is the resolution act.

1. It tells how the protagonist reaches his goal or is ennobled by his effort.

Chapter 11 shows you how to create the crucial shifts that carry the audience from one act to the next. These two change points are the most critical junctures of any movie. And as you may have guessed, they too are reversals — reversals on steroids — and need a chapter all to themselves.

Chapter 11
Act Reversals

The two most important turning points in your screenplay are the first and second act reversals.

During one of the first semesters I taught screenwriting, I was babbling on about films being nothing like real life. "After all," I said, "In every six or seven minute segment of your life you don't have a conflict-reversal, another conflict-reversal, and then even more conflict-reversal." At that point a woman blurted out, "Oh, then you must not be married."

One of the most difficult aspects of writing a producible script is making your narrative (though a complete contrivance) seem realistic. The scripts that best accomplish this feat are those with well-structured scenes and a clear and smoothly rendered three-act structure.

In Chapter 10, we covered how to write a clear three-act structure. To achieve the *smoothly rendered* part, we need to examine the staples that bind these acts together. They are act reversals.

Each scene has a reversal, so too, does each act. In fact, act reversals are nothing more than scene reversals that assume, by plot and placement, a superior role in your script. I often compare act reversals to the prime minister in a parliamentary government. Even though the prime minister is the head of her party, she must stand for election from her particular district just as all the other party members do. So in one sense, the prime minister is just another member of parliament. But in reality, she assumes a far more important role as the leader of her nation.

Act reversals are the most important reversals in an act. So as we did with the three-act structure in the previous chapter, let's start with the mathematics of these reversals and then tackle their definitions and objectives.

Act Reversals

There are two act reversals in a script. The first appears near the end of the first act, usually between pages 23 and 28. The second appears approximately three-quarters of the way through the script, usually between pages 73 and 88, but most often somewhere in the 80s.

Even for shorter feature-length scripts, the first-act reversal often emerges around page 28. *Men in Black*, for instance, is a 98 minute movie, but the first act reversal takes place at 28 minutes and 27 seconds into the film. Since all the elements comprising a film must be introduced in Act I, it often takes thirty minutes just to acquaint the audience with everyone and everything contained within it.

What is an act reversal?

An act reversal is the point in the act at which the direction and emotion (secondary and primary) changes, taking the story in a different direction.

An act reversal does for an act what a scene reversal does for a scene. An act reversal must

1. Change the direction of the act

2. Change the emotions of the protagonist, antagonist, and/or the audience

3. Be a surprise, but a logical surprise, to the protagonist, antagonist, and/or the audience

4. Propel the story into the next act

5. Make the reader anxious to discover what will happen next

An act reversal spins the act in a new direction. However, since it comes just before the end of the act, the characters and the audience have a chance to respond to the action before moving on.

Both the first and second act reversals involve the protagonist, but the first act reversal must fulfill different criteria from the second act reversal. How you handle these two act reversals and their criteria will go a long way toward determining the success of your protagonist and your screenplay. To clarify this statement, let's look at these two reversals separately.

In the first act reversal, one (and only one) of the following three story developments must take place:

1. The protagonist makes a decision.

2. A decision is made for the protagonist.

3. The protagonist and antagonist experience their first significant meeting. (This does not necessarily have to be the first encounter between the two, which is usually casual and by chance. The reversal meeting binds the protagonist and antagonist to each other so that the actions of one affect the conduct of the other.)

A note of caution: You may use only one of these three story developments as the first act reversal. So choose it wisely, because this reversal will affect the rest of your script.

Let's study examples from twelve movies. The first four examples depict the protagonist making a decision, the second four depict a decision being made for the protagonist, and the final four describe the first significant meeting between protagonist and antagonist. All twelve reversals in both the first and second acts of these films clearly depict a change of direction, a change of emotion, a surprise to the characters and/or the audience, a segue around a literal or figurative dead end, and a push or jump into the next act. Because these are successful films, we know that the audiences who watched them remained in their seats, anxious to discover what would happen next.

The films are

1. *Ordinary People*
2. *Star Wars*
3. *The Sixth Sense*
4. *The Aviator*
5. *Toy Story*
6. *Dave*
7. *Top Gun*
8. *Million Dollar Baby*
9. *E.T.*
10. *Back to the Future*
11. *Shakespeare in Love*
12. *Sideways*

Option 1 - The Protagonist Makes a Decision

Ordinary People: Calvin suggests to his son, Conrad, that he call Dr. Berger, a psychiatrist with a stellar reputation. It is not until a quarter of the way through the film, at the first act reversal, that Conrad decides to go see Dr. Berger.

Star Wars: Obie Wan asks Luke to join him in the quest to save the Princess. Luke makes excuses at first, but accepts Obie Wan's challenge after witnessing the deaths of his aunt and uncle at the hands of the Empire.

The Sixth Sense: After reviewing a previous case in which he failed to help a patient who had problems similar to his new patient, Malcolm decides he will listen, learn, and try to help Cole Sear.

The Aviator: Howard Hughes decides to buy controlling interest in TWA.

Option 2 - A Decision is Made For the Protagonist

Toy Story: Woody, who is playing a trick on Buzz to make him fall between the bed and the wall so Andy will take him to Pizza Planet instead of Buzz, actually causes Buzz to be pushed out the window and fall into the yard.

Dave: After the President suffers a debilitating heart attack, Dave is chosen as his replacement.

Top Gun: Maverick is chosen to attend Top Gun School.

Million Dollar Baby: Big Willie leaves Frankie for a different trainer/manager.

Option 3 - The First Significant Meeting Between the Protagonist and Antagonist

E.T.: Elliot and E.T. connect emotionally and psychologically after E.T. brings Elliot the Reese's Pieces.

Back to the Future: Marty meets his future father in the soda shop.

Shakespeare in Love: Viola, dressed as a young man, meets William while auditioning for one of his plays.

Sideways: Miles and Jack inadvertently meet up with Maya after dinner.

Jack concludes that Maya likes Miles and wants to see more of him. Jack arranges a date a short time later.

Now let's examine an act reversal in a film from each of our three options, and determine if they meet the five criteria needed to satisfy an act reversal.

1: The Protagonist Makes a Decision

The Sixth Sense: Should Malcolm refuse to help Cole in recompense for being unable to help his former patient, he will forego the opportunity to make amends for his tragic mistake and, ultimately, the ability to understand his own predicament.

When Malcolm verbally declares that he will help Cole, his life moves in a new direction.

Malcolm gives himself and the audience new hope that this time he will get it right and find a way to help his patient.

Malcolm surprises the audience. He had been treating Cole identically to his former patient, Vincent. But he surprises himself with his insight into Cole's condition, and is able to craft a treatment for and forge a relationship with the boy that carries into the next two acts. It also gives Malcolm his first opportunity to practice psychiatry after his premature retirement.

The audience wants to see if Malcolm can stay true to his word and find a way to help Cole Sear.

2: A Decision is Made For the Protagonist

Million Dollar Baby: Frankie is making plans for a title fight for Big Willie. Big Willie tells Frankie that he's leaving Frankie for another manager.

It is obvious that Frankie's desire to train a boxer for a championship fight is second only to reconciling with his daughter. We, along with Frankie, are disappointed and a bit angry when Willie leaves.

Even though Frankie had been warned by Scrap that Willie was "not talking" to another manager, Frankie seems shocked and upset over Willie leaving.

We wonder what Frankie will do. Will he finally decide to take on Maggie?

We want to stay around to find out the answer.

3: The First Significant Meeting Between the Protagonist and Antagonist

Shakespeare in Love: Will is despondent because he can't find an actor talented enough to play Romeo when Viola, disguised as a man named Thomas, auditions for the role and wins the part.

Will rejoices that he has finally found a terrific actor who can handle the role, but when he asks Viola to remove her hat, she runs off.

Will so badly wants Viola to perform in his play that he follows her to her house.

His pursuit surprises Viola as well as the audience.

Will's method of gaining admittance to Viola's house for a dance that night leads to a relationship which helps him break his writer's block and makes us anticipate the film's resolution.

Your turn. Take the other nine films (or almost any Hollywood film produced after 1969) and decide on the protagonist and antagonist.

Then find the first act reversal and decide which of the three story options we explored gives the best fit. Finally, decide how the act reversal successfully meets our five criteria. By learning and practicing with existing films, you will be better able to plan your own first act reversal during the outline phase of your script. Once you get it nailed down, you will be well on your way toward producing a clear blueprint for your next film script.

Second Act Reversal

What about the second act reversal? Glad you asked.

The second act reversal foreshadows the events of the third act and belongs solely to the protagonist. It is her time to shine, to take control, to oppose the slings and arrows of outrageous fortune. Even though the protagonist may have been a pawn in some cosmic chess game even this far into the script, the second act reversal will change all that. The protagonist may gradually begin to assume control over certain facets of her life in Act II, but the second act reversal will show beyond a doubt that the protagonist will now make every decision, direct every movement, and take responsibility for her every action.

The second act reversal is the point at which the protagonist makes a decision to take charge of his life regardless of the outcome. Think of it this way: Since the protagonist is the person who changes the most, what greater change can a character in a film (or in real life for that matter) make than to finally say, 'I'm in charge no matter what, and I am completely responsible for whatever happens.' There are presidents, world leaders, and people we know personally who have never achieved that level of awareness and probably never will.

In most movies, the protagonist decides that he will finish the job on his own terms regardless of the outcome — be it triumph, nobility, or even death. Let's look at six of the listed films to see how the second act reversal plays out.

Star Wars: Luke's decision to attack the Death Star is do-or-die. He will either succeed or be destroyed.

The Sixth Sense: Malcolm discovers the source of Cole's problem as well as that of his former patient, Vincent. More importantly, if he is able to help Cole solve his problem, he will have partially made amends for his past failure.

Toy Story: Woody appeals to all of Sid's toys to help him rescue Buzz. When they agree, Woody formulates and successfully directs a plan of action.

Top Gun: Maverick chooses to graduate from Top Gun School.

Back to the Future: Real simple. George stands up to Biff and defeats him. Lorraine is smitten and as a result, they get together at the dance and Marty gets to stay in existence.

Sideways: Miles tells Maya about Jack's wedding. This is one of his first attempts at honesty. Although he is not completely there yet, he is heading in a better direction.

Take a stab at the rest of the listed films or any other Hollywood film. Once you begin to pinpoint the act reversals in the movies you watch, you will be able to plan them in your own scripts.

There are other major turning points on this journey through your script. We'll discuss those points in Chapter 12.

Chapter 12
Turn, Turn, Turn

There are five other major turning points and the script contact point (opening) that are critical for guiding you through the three-act structure.

Imagine that you're driving from Baltimore to L.A., starting and arriving at specific dates. Now imagine that you make stops in Washington D.C., Louisville, St. Louis, Kansas City, Denver, and Las Vegas, also at specific dates.

The journey through the three-act structure employs a similar scenario. Knowing where you must begin (script contact point) and when and how you need to arrive at the seven major turning points will help make your script focused, smooth, and much more manageable.

We have studied two of these seven turning points — the *first and second act reversals* — but there are five other critical points and the script contact point we must also visit. Think of them as oases in the desert that will give your script renewed strength and sustenance.

They are

Script Contact Point (the opening)
First Scene Reversal
Story Set Point
Middle Reversal
Resolution
Ending

Script Contact Point (The Opening)

A question I'm often asked in my screenwriting classes is "Where do I begin my screenplay?" The smart-alack answer is that you begin at the beginning. But the beginning requires special attention because it's crucial to leave the reader with a good first impression of your script.

Many agents and producers will tell you that you must hook the reader within the first fifteen pages of your script. I think this is a generous estimate. Most readers decide within the first few pages, eight to ten tops, if your work is worthwhile. So openings matter. And it is the *first contact point* and the *first scene reversal* that usually determine the fate of your script.

First Contact Point

Begin your script just before your protagonist's "normal" life changes. You can do this in two different ways: You may start off by depicting your protagonist in "Normal Mode." In other words, what his life is like the moment before the event that changes his destiny happens. The other method is to foreshadow the change in your protagonist by depicting previous events that will ultimately bring about his transformation. Let's look at examples of both methods.

Normal Mode

In *Silence of the Lambs*, Clarice is attacking an obstacle course, pushing hard to be the best cadet in her class.

In *The Sixth Sense*, Dr. Malcolm Crowe and his wife are celebrating an award he received for his achievements in child psychology and his efforts to help children and their families.

In *Erin Brockovich*, Erin is seeking employment.

In *A Beautiful Mind*, John Nash sits in a classroom with his classmates, listening to his teacher encourage them to become the Einsteins of their generation by using their math skills to help win the Cold War.

How Events Elsewhere Will Change the Protagonist

In *Back to the Future*, Marty is visiting his scientist friend, Dr. Brown. Marty receives a phone call from Dr. Brown that will ultimately change everything for Marty's father, George.

After school, when Marty comes home, we see what "Normal Mode" is for George.

In *Men in Black*, Kay's partner isn't able to shoot the Alien. This incident will have a dramatic effect on James' future.

First Scene Reversal

The *first scene reversal* is the incident or event that initiates a change in the protagonist and steers him down a new path. Remember the graphic in Chapter 7 showing the protagonist heading toward a new goal? It is the reversal in the first scene — or at the very latest by page 10 — where the protagonist is pulled from his original goal and begins the journey toward a changed fate. This first scene reversal has also been labeled the *inciting incident*, the *shift*, the *precipitating event*. Whatever you label it, it is the catalyst that brings together the many disparate elements of a script — people, events, or objects — that otherwise might never mesh, mix, or meet in the same universe.

The incident can be as simple as a phone call or as traumatic as the death of a loved one. It can be as spectacular as the arrival of aliens from outer space or as mundane as a chance meeting that will ultimately bring two dissimilar characters together. It can be as routine as a detective being assigned to a new case, or in a romantic comedy, as innocuous as when the romantic leads meet or notice each other for the first time.

The first scene reversal is the event that starts the wheels turning, the dominoes falling (however you might define it); it is what disrupts the norm, moves the Mojo, engages the Karma and forces the protagonist onto a different path and headed toward a new goal. The protagonist may not realize it at the time — and may never realize it — but this is the event that will turn his world on its axis.

Let's examine some film examples to see how the first scene reversal altered the norm.

In *Back To The Future*, Marty gets a phone call from Dr. Brown asking Marty to meet him at Twin Pines Shopping Mall late that night and to bring the box under the table. This initiates a series of events that will drastically alter George McFly's life.

In *Silence of the Lambs*, Clarice is assigned the "interesting errand" of meeting and interviewing Hannibal Lector.

In *The Sixth Sense*, a former patient that Malcolm failed to help changes Malcolm's life and goals.

In *Erin Brockovich*, Erin is injured after being struck by a car following a job interview. She goes to Ed Masry, a lawyer who will ultimately bring about a huge change in her life and in the lives and fortunes of hundreds of other people.

In *A Beautiful Mind*, John Nash realizes that he's competing against others who, unlike himself, went to the finest prep schools and have already made a name for themselves. He believes that in order to distinguish himself, he must find and develop a truly original idea.

Sometimes the reversal occurs before the story opens, and the ripple effects change your characters' destiny. For example:

In *War Games*, the soldier refuses to turn the key — the key that could start World War III — and the army decides to turn over their entire nuclear missile launch sequence to a computer program designed and developed by the "late" Dr. Falken.

In *Witness*, Rachel's husband has died. To escape a suitor she doesn't want and a situation she wants to put behind her, she decides that she and her son will travel to Baltimore to visit relatives. It is on that trip her son will witness a murder that will change everything for her and John Book.

In *Dead Poets Society*, the academy has hired a new English teacher who will have a profound affect on many of his students, especially Todd.

What were the first scene reversals in the last several films you saw? Can't remember? Look for them in the next movies you see. Analyze and assess them. What you learn will help you discover and write your own first scene reversals.

The first scene reversal plays such a consequential role because, like the first and second act reversals, it changes the direction of the story. It wrenches the protagonist from his normal life and affects everything that happens afterwards. The first scene reversal must be emphatic, logical, and an obvious change for your hero and/or your audience. It must be the surge that carries everything and everyone in your script to its conclusion.

Story Set Point

The *story set point* is the turning point in your script where the main plot line becomes evident. It occurs somewhere around the middle of the first act (usually about page 15) after most of the major characters have been introduced. It tells what the story is about and the direction in which it's headed.

In *Raiders of the Lost Ark*, we are told that the Nazis are seeking the Ark. A few minutes later Indy is commissioned to find the Ark before the Nazis do.

In *The Sixth Sense*, Dr. Malcolm Crowe emerges from semi-retirement to take on a new patient, eight-year-old Cole Sear.

In *Erin Brockovich*, Erin is hired by the Masry and Vititoe law firm.

In *A Beautiful Mind*, John Nash hints at the theory that will ultimately win him the Nobel Prize. He suggests to Charles, his "roommate", that there may be a way to create a system in competitive situations where there are no losers.

In *Sideways*, Jack tells Miles his plans for them during their week in the wine country.

In *Million Dollar Baby*, Frankie doesn't want Maggie to work out at his gym, but he can't afford to return the six months worth of dues she has paid.

Middle Reversal

The *middle act reversal* is the event that pulls the protagonist across a threshold and places her in a situation where she must adapt to a new and changing environment. At this turning point, events control the protagonist instead of the other way around.

It is in Act II part 1 that the protagonist's problems increase in number, complexity, and most unsettling, intensity. Before this turning point, the protagonist is still able to escape her situation and return to her normal (or almost normal) life. The middle reversal closes that final escape hatch.

Let's look at some examples of middle act reversals.

In *Witness*, John Book's partner tells him during a phone call that conditions are too hot to return to Philadelphia, and that the police are blaming him (John) for the murder of the cop. To keep out of sight and protect Samuel and Rachel, John stays at the Lapp's.

In *Back to the Future*, Marty, disguised as Darth Vader, persuades George to ask Lorraine to the dance.

In *The Firm*, the detective's secretary tells Mitch about the men who killed her boss.

Near the middle of *Men in Black*, Kay and Jay discover the identity and species of Edgar the Bug. Kay realizes they must find and stop Edgar in order to save planet Earth.

In *A Beautiful Mind*, John tries to quit spying for Parcher, but Parcher threatens John and his wife.

In *Million Dollar Baby*, Frankie takes over as Maggie's trainer/manager in the middle of a fight and tells her afterward that he will never again leave her.

Enhance the importance of the middle reversal by writing a situation immediately preceding it that will make the audience desperate to find out what will happen next. Pretend that there will be an intermission (or worse, a commercial) in your film, and you need to give your audience a good reason to return from the snack bar. You must make this situation so exciting, intriguing, engaging, or compelling that your audience can't wait for the second half to begin. Let's see if our examples accomplished this goal.

In *Witness*, John Book is near death and being cared for by the Lapps. He realizes while recovering that he will be killed or jailed if he returns to Philadelphia to reveal the identity of the murderer. How will he bring the corrupt cops to justice?

In *Back to the Future*, George has convinced himself that he's no good with girls and that Lorraine will never go to the dance with him. It becomes a matter of life and death for Marty to convince George to ask her to the dance.

In *The Firm*, Mitch realizes that something is wrong with his dream job and that he must escape his situation in order to survive.

In *Men in Black*, Kay knows that a crisis is brewing, but he must consult the "hot sheets" to discover his next lead.

In *A Beautiful Mind*, John, believing he has been pursued and almost killed, thinks he and his family are at risk. He wants out of his job as a spy.

In *Million Dollar Baby*, Maggie is getting beat in the ring. Frankie is watching and wincing each time she leaves herself open by dropping her left.

The middle reversal gives you something to work toward (and spin away from) in the long and involved second act. It is an exciting and provocative juncture that will increase the momentum of your story and re-energize your script as you transition into the second half of your screenplay.

One semantic note: Some screenwriting instructors refer to the middle reversal as an act reversal. They claim that a film consists of four acts instead of three, and the middle reversal is the point at which the second act transitions into the third. The problem with this reasoning is that, unlike the first and second act reversals which occur at the end of the first and second acts, the middle reversal need not be in the exact middle of your script, and may fall anywhere between pages 45 and 60. In effect, it divides the second act into two parts, Act II part 1, and Act II part 2.

Resolution and Ending

The last two major turning points, the *resolution* and *ending*, show up at or near the end of Act III. This may seem simple and obvious, but there's more to these points than you might first imagine.

The protagonist and the audience enter the final act via the second act reversal. As I described previously, this is the point where the protagonist stops being pushed around and starts doing some pushing of her own. It's a change in attitude, perspective, and purpose. And it's the third act resolution that confirms the actions and stance the protagonist took at the end of Act II.

The resolution occurs near the end of Act III and can almost be defined as a third act reversal. Simply put, the resolution is the point or scene in which the protagonist either achieves his goal or is ennobled in the effort.

In *Star Wars*, Luke destroys the Death Star.

In *Witness*, John Book captures the murderer.

In *E.T.*, Elliot helps E.T. return to his fellow beings.

In *Erin Brockovich*, Erin finds the internal memos that prove that the utility company's main office knew about the contamination of the Hinkley water, and that they tried to hide the facts from the public.

In *Men in Black*, Jay and Kay, with the help of Dr. Weaver, stop Edgar from leaving planet Earth and retrieve the fought-over Galaxy.

In *Million Dollar Baby*, Frankie makes the most difficult decision of his life.

While the resolution reveals how the protagonist achieves her goal, the *ending* provides evidence that achieving that goal has brought about a lasting change in the protagonist. It is the ending that provides the audience with visual and sometimes verbal confirmation that the change in the protagonist is permanent.

In *Witness*, it's when Eli tells John Book, "You be careful out there among the English."

In *Back to the Future*, it's George McFly bossing Biff, getting his first novel published, having classier furniture, etc.

In *Star Wars* it's Luke Skywalker being decorated for leading the Rebels against Darth Vader and the Death Star.

In *Erin Brockovich*, it's when Ed tells Erin that he had to adjust her bonus money for the work she performed. Erin, believing that Ed intends to give her less than he originally intended, protests until Ed hands her a two million dollar check. Now Erin is floored and doesn't know what to say. Ed asks her if they teach beauty queens how to apologize because she sucks at it.

In *Men in Black*, it's when Jay assumes the job that previously belonged to Kay.

In *Sideways*, it's when Miles takes a chance by going to see Maya.

Films that do not end happily-ever-after demonstrate that even if the protagonist doesn't achieve his goal, there is nobility in the effort. Films such as *Twelve Monkeys*, *Steel Magnolias*, *Million Dollar Baby*, and *The Aviator* have tragic or bittersweet endings. Never-the-less, the nobility of the quest and of our protagonist is clear and decisive.

While openings leave first impressions, endings leave lasting ones. As the above examples show, it doesn't take much time to confirm a permanent change in the protagonist. The ending (visually and/or verbally) confirms that the change in the protagonist is permanent.

Knowing the intermediate stops in your journey and your time of arrival at each of them are critical to success. Planning these points before you begin writing and inserting them into your scene outline are important steps in guiding you and your characters safely through the three-act structure.

Chapter 13
Small Packages

These are three minor points that can mean a lot to your protagonist, your antagonist, and the success of your screenplay.

The *low point*, the *baring of the soul*, and the *climax* are three small but important points that you must account for when writing your screenplay. These points always appear in the second half of the script, always after the mid-point reversal and usually at the end of the second act or in Act III.

Low Point

The *low point* is the point in your screenplay where it seems that the protagonist, despite his valiant efforts, will be unable to succeed in his quest, and that nobility is all that he will be capable of achieving because his new goal seems impossible to reach.

In the third act of *Star Wars*, as Luke maneuvers in to destroy the Death Star, R2D2 has been put out of commission, Luke's two support ships have been blown out of the sky, and Darth Vader is right on Luke's backside. At this point, it appears that Luke will never be able defeat the Empire.

Near the end of *Men In Black*, it appears Jay won't be able to keep Edgar the Bug from leaving the planet.

In the third act of *Erin Brockovich*, while it seems that Erin may get enough people to sign on to the class action suit, she will not be able to get the information she needs to prove that the chief officers of the utility company knew that the water was being poisoned.

Toward the end of *Million Dollar Baby*, it seems that Frankie can't help Maggie, or do anything to eliminate her misery.

Baring of the Soul

The *baring of the soul* is the point in your script where the protagonist speaks the truth about himself or his situation. This doesn't necessarily mean that the protagonist is speaking the actual truth; he may lack critical information about his situation or may simply be deceiving himself. But it *is* the point where the protagonist speaks the truth as he knows it, and is able to honestly express his true feelings to himself and to the audience.

In *Star Wars* at the end of Act II, Luke tells Han Solo how he feels about Han's refusal to join them in the quest to destroy the Death Star.

In *Men in Black*, Jay and Kay have a short talk after destroying Edgar. Kay indicates that he wants to retire. Jay says that he can't handle the job by himself.

In the second act of *Erin Brockovich*, Ed Masry becomes angry with Erin when she accuses him of not working hard enough. He tells her of the illnesses and surgeries he suffered through while building his firm and saving for retirement.

In Act III of *Million Dollar Baby*, Frankie discusses his dilemma over Maggie's condition with Father Horvath.

This is one of the few times in the script when the protagonist can be a little more talky and truthful, and is the one occasion where you might use a short soliloquy to give him a bit more space and time to speak his mind. It should not be long or tedious, however, but afford your character with a reflective moment to express some bottled up emotions, and give the audience the opportunity to gain a deeper understanding of the character.

Climax

In literature, the *climax* and *resolution* are often the same. In film there is a difference. We already know the resolution is the scene in which the protagonist achieves his goal, or if unsuccessful, is at least ennobled in the effort. The dramatic climax is the last real encounter between the protagonist and antagonist, and it usually appears just before the resolution in the third act. This does not necessarily mean a showdown or a fight — it can be a struggle of minds or wills, or a contest of strength.

In *Star Wars*, as the rebel ships approach the Death Star, Darth Vader says "The Force is strong in this one."

In *Chinatown*, Jake asks Noah Cross why he wants to control the water supply in Los Angeles given that he has all the money he needs. Noah says it's not about having money, it's about having power.

In *Men In Black*, Kay tells Jay that he (Kay) is retiring.

And in *Million Dollar Baby*, Maggie asks Frankie for one last, gut-wrenching favor.

My students sometimes ask if they should keep the entire Hollywood Script Structure in mind when planning and writing their script. My answer is that these points are an essential part of the fabric of any screenplay. Whether you're deciding how to write your first-act reversal, planning your middle reversal, or wrapping up the climax of your story, your knowledge of the three-act structure and the turning points in that structure are essential.

While breaking the rules may be your ultimate goal, you'll be unable to break them intelligently without first being able to learn and implement the rules of the Hollywood Script Structure. It is an indispensable ingredient for planning, writing, and completing your screenplay.

Chapter 14
Can We Talk   Part 1

Film-speak is not communication, it is miscommunication.

Shortly before his company introduced the first talking motion picture in 1927, Jack Warner said, "Who the hell wants to hear actors talk?" Obviously, most moviegoers do. On-screen dialogue saved Warner Brothers, and it can enhance your filmscripts if you understand when and how to use it.

When should we use dialogue? The answer seems simple. We use dialogue when characters need to speak. But characters don't need to speak as often as many screenwriters believe. Film is still primarily a visual medium. And a general rule for talk vs. action is that a movie script should contain no more than forty percent dialogue. This means that at least sixty percent of your script should be slugs and direction.

I realize that there are screenwriters who have successfully broken this rule. However, many industry professionals believe that excessive dialogue in a script results in a film heavily dependent on verbal rather than visual communication. And that means a "talky" film.

One way to use dialogue to improve, rather than encumber, your script is to recognize that dialogue should be used in only three situations:

To reveal some characterization that cannot be shown

To reveal some exposition that cannot be shown

To reveal conflict between or among characters

If your dialogue does not meet one of these three criteria, dump it. Small talk such as "How are you?" and "Fine, thank you." does nothing to tell us about character or exposition, and it certainly doesn't indicate conflict.

Be careful as well of superfluous phone and meeting room dialogue. One of my favorite phone conversations in film is from *A Thousand Clowns*. Murray picks up the ringing phone and instead of saying hello, asks, "Is this someone with good news or money?" When the answer is negative, he hangs up. This dialogue is short, funny, to the point, and tells us a lot about Murray.

Let's next consider how we use dialogue. One prominent acting theory asserts that each character in a scene is trying to be the best or the smartest or the most knowledgeable or the top dog or the bravest or the strongest or the cleverest. In other words, each is trying to win something in the scene. Therefore, everything each character does — action, reaction, body language, and dialogue — is done to achieve that goal.

One of the best ways screenwriters can show this dynamic is by having their characters talk *at* and not *with* each other. Thus, Character A uses dialogue to gain an advantage over Character B, and B then manipulates it some more to regain the advantage. This type of dialogue creates conflict, and more conflict means better movie-speak.

How do we develop dialogue that is situation-oriented but character driven? How do we formulate dialogue that compels characters to talk at and not with each other? How do we compose the kind of exchange that does not hinder the plot but adds something extra to a dynamic and compelling story?

First, be careful about permitting characters to respond to direct questions. A character who gives a yes or no answer to a question is essentially allowing the character asking the question to retain the advantage. Not only does this not win the scene, it thoroughly loses it.

For example, if Character A asks a question, Character B, instead of answering yes or no, might respond with a question of his own. Someone challenged me in class one night, "Suppose I asked you, do you like ice cream? How would you answer?"

I thought a moment and said, "You're buying?"

Even in courtroom situations, the fewer yeses and nos, the better off you and your characters will be.

The best way to pen moviespeak's special brand of miscommunication is to use a system I call *A-B dialogue*. This system is really a series of exercises that use your writing ability, your ear for language, your imagination, and even your acting skill to create compelling and realistic dialogue.

Begin the A-B dialogue when your scene is already outlined and analyzed. You know what the scene is about, what the conflict is, and especially, what the reversal will be. In fact, you know already how you'll use all seven elements needed to create an effective scene. You've also set a tentative number of pages for the scene as well as labeled your reversal. Finally, you know what emotion you want your audience to feel, and you've done your best to ensure your audience will respond emotionally the way you want it to. All that's left is dialogue.

For the sake of simplicity, I will assume there are only two characters in this particular scene. Also for simplicity sake, and for the A-B dialogue namesake, I will call one Character A and the other B. A is so labeled because he may have slightly more to do, more lines, or be slightly more important.

First, sit at a desk, pen in hand (try to avoid using the computer in this exercise) with three sheets of colored 8.5 x 14 legal paper in front of you. Use this paper so the A-B exercise won't get buried and lost among all the other paper you use to write your script.

Now pretend you are Character A. In fact, instead of pretending, use your imagination and acting ability to actually become Character A. As Character A, you know what you want to achieve or accomplish in this scene. You know how you will behave, act, react, and try to win the scene.

Next, relax, open your mind, and clear it of any outside thoughts. Go into your character zone and prepare to brainstorm. Now, as quickly as possible and without stopping, write down every phrase, line, or sentence that you might say in that scene. Don't worry about whether your lines make sense or have anything to do with the scene. Do not stop to think about problems or solutions. Do not censor yourself. Even if a line seems so out of place that you have no idea where it came from or where it would fit into your scene, write it down anyway — non-sequiturs can sometimes be the perfect replies in a dialogue sequence. Just keep writing lines, phrases, and words until all three pages — one side only — are filled.

Once you have finished with Character A, take a rest. Get up and stretch or exercise. Go catch a movie, visit friends, watch some TV, or do whatever it takes to relax for a while. When you return, you will assume another role. As you may have guessed, you will become Character B.

As Character B, you will have pen or pencil in hand with three sheets of legal-size paper. Again, you know what you want to achieve or accomplish in this scene. You know how you will think, act, and react. So relax, open your mind, and get those words, phrases, and sentences on paper as soon as they jump into your head.

Remember! Respond only as Character B would. You cannot and should not react to anything A might do or say because you are not Character A, you are Character B. As Character B, finish the pages and again relax for a while. When you return to your script, it will be time to produce the first draft of your scene.

The first item you add to your scene will be the primary slug, followed, most likely, by one or more paragraphs of direction. Somewhere in the scene, though, dialogue happens. This is where those pages of A and B dialogue you brainstormed come into play.

Okay, A speaks first. What does A say? Look through your three sheets and find a word, phrase, sentence, or combination of words, phrases, or sentences. Maybe a sentence in the middle of page one and a phrase from the bottom of page two can be put together for a snappy, strong, or stinging first speech.

How will B reply? Look through your sheets and find a word, phrase, sentence, or combination to rejoin. Maybe something from the top of page two is the perfect comeback.

Continue using your sheets for all the dialogue contained in the scene. Of course, you will not use anywhere near everything you have written on the A-B pages.

The purpose of creating A-B dialogue is two-fold. First, (as we have discussed) to maneuver the conversation back toward each character's objective, and second, to maintain each character's distinct voice.

Many of my students want to skip the exercises with A-B dialogue. Some students believe they already write great dialogue and need no further help. Others feel the exercise takes too long and hinders work on the script. A few believe if the characters are strong and true, the dialogue will take care of itself.

Let me answer those three oft-heard objections.

First, yes it's true that a few of my students — a very few — have been naturals at film-speak. Most have not. Students forget that film dialogue is meant to be manipulative and to create conflict. Because this is not the kind of dialogue we usually engage in on a daily basis, it's only through practice that we can achieve good movie discourse. And it's through A-B dialogue that you will successfully make the transition from everyday talk to film-speak.

What about all the time it takes to do this exercise? I admit, A-B dialogue is labor intensive. The first time I tried it, I spent an hour and forty-five minutes on it from start to completion. But subsequent attempts took shorter amounts of time until it came almost in a flash. After you've worked with the A-B process several times, you will eventually learn to recognize it quickly in the movies you watch and compose it more easily in the scripts you write.

Another element to keep in mind is that the time investment in A-B dialogue is worthwhile. After all, good, sharp dialogue is almost as essential to your script as terrific plot and characters. Why work long and hard on sixty plus percent of your script and shrug off the rest because of a little extra time? You know the saying: *there is never time to do something right but always time to do it over.*

Finally, do great characters automatically create great dialogue? (And you get no popcorn, drink, and candy combo for this answer.) Let's face it, for the vast majority of us, creating great characters saying wonderful, weighty, or witty things does not happen by accident. Since most Hollywood film is built on plot and story, the dialogue first needs to reflect the conflict in the plot and story that A-B dialogue promotes. And the A-B exercise can help you write that pithy, sharp speech between your characters, which, of course, makes the script that much stronger.

The A-B technique is the best method that I've seen for producing real film-speak as opposed to just lines a bunch of characters hang around and deliver. I've seen A-B dialogue help many students and greatly improve countless scripts. I urge you to try it a few times, if not more often. You'll be pleasantly surprised at the improved quality of your own scripts.

In the next chapter, we cover other methods of trimming and improving dialogue: *dialogue surgery*, *avoiding the ten biggest dialogue glitches*, and *using your own listening talents*. So on to Chapter 15.

Chapter 15
Can We Talk Part II

Film dialogue needs surgery, and you must be the surgeon.

What lines do you remember from movies? From *Casablanca*, maybe just about every one, but with most films — including *Casablanca* — the lines commonly quoted are usually the short, pithy ones.

Think about it. Paddy Chayefsky, one of our most brilliant playwrights and screenwriters, wrote several hits, including *The Americanization of Emily*, *Altered States*, and *Marty*. In *The Americanization of Emily*, James Garner delivers some wonderful tongue-in-cheek pro-war speeches. They are well done, extremely clever. I always ask my students if they can quote any of those speeches. No one has yet. But what *can* you quote from Chayefsky? How about from *Network*? All together now: "I'm mad as hell, and I'm not going to take this anymore."

To make the argument for short, pithy dialogue even stronger, let's look at Noel Coward. He is considered one of our greatest dialogue writers. Can you quote me anything of his? (So far there has been only one taker on this.) But I'll bet you can quote me something by Dirty Harry Callahan. How about James Bond? Tarzan? E.T.? Of course you know those. Those lines were pointed, pithy, and powerful. It doesn't take as much dialogue as you think for a scene or a script to be successful. Less is more, and if you don't believe that, "Go ahead, make your competitor's day."

In the last chapter, I discussed the need for applying the A-B dialogue technique. In this chapter, we will delve into performing dialogue surgery, avoiding the ten most common dialogue glitches, and using your own listening talents. These three practices, combined with A-B dialogue, will give you the best chance of creating dialogue that is strong and concise. Let's begin with dialogue surgery.

It is vital to recognize that the look of your screenplay indicates the pace and style of the film itself and often determines whether a script is given serious consideration. So shaping and streamlining your conversations are a vital step in making each page of your script look and read like the professional work it needs to be.

One of the first ways to clean up your script is to identify and eliminate *talking heads*. What are talking heads? Successive pages of dialogue without action are talking heads. One of my students, who initially wrote dialogue as if he were being paid by the word, led me to develop a rule of thumb to help solve this problem. Write no more than a page to a page-and-a-half of unbroken dialogue per scene. (And I don't mean after a page of dialogue, stick in one or two lines of direction and continue the dialogue for another page or more.) This guideline helped my student to purge unnecessary dialogue and (as an added attraction) sell some screenplays. No matter how witty the banter, a character who chats incessantly — which may play well in live theater or even on television — will generally kill a film.

Another problem is that many beginning writers create individual character speeches that are too long. Minimize this problem by limiting most speeches to no more than four lines. Admittedly, limits of four lines per speech and a page to a page-and-a-half of continuous dialogue are arbitrary. But in the process of imposing these restrictions, you'll come to understand two important aspects of dialogue: 1) it is possible to say too much, and 2) it is possible to eliminate a lot of excess dialogue and still say exactly what you need to say in a better and more efficient manner.

Don't worry that following these guidelines will make your dialogue too austere. In all the scripts that I have critiqued, both from students and writers around the country, I have rarely encountered a script in which the dialogue was too sparse. Even when I felt the prose was too minimalist, and it was difficult at times to understand the action in the script, the dialogue itself was not so spartan as to be incomprehensible.

Dialogue almost always errs in excess. Too much is repeated, writers tell instead of show, exposition overkill dominates, and the writer tries to accomplish far too much with each individual speech.

One way to break these habits is to place a one subject limit on each paragraph of dialogue. Again, this is a guideline and not a mandate. Limiting each speech to one specific topic or thought will force you (and your character) to focus on what that particular speech needs to achieve. It also limits the amount of dialogue required to satisfy that objective.

Another reason to keep dialogue focused is to keep your high-power lines from being diminished by the other sentences around it. "Go ahead, make my day" is potent stuff. "Go ahead, make my day. Shoot the woman. What do I care? You're the one I'm after. I'll enjoy pulling the trigger on you, punk." is overkill (pun intended) and ineffective.

Sticking to one subject and practicing word economy are the best ways to keep your dialogue crisp, focused, and forceful. Your characters will still say what you want them to say, but they'll say it with shorter and far more dynamic speeches.

Once you've shortened your speeches, learn to practice good word economy through more specific dialogue surgery.

How do you perform this specific surgery? First, cutting fillers such as *well, sure, uh, yeah, gee, of course, like, hey, you know, oh,* and similar phrases is a good place to start. They add nothing to dialogue but excess. Use them if it helps to get the words on paper, but eliminate them in subsequent drafts.

There is one exception: If one of your characters distinguishes herself by the use of one of these phrases, keep it.

Second, watch for redundant prepositions that do nothing for your script but lengthen the dialogue. For instance

>PROFESSOR JOHN
>I discovered early on in this course that she had talent.

>DEPARTMENT HEAD CAL
>Later on, we went fishing.

>PRINCIPAL SAL
>Before I could get a word in edgewise, he started up the car.

I could continue on — I mean continue — but I believe you get the point. How does *early on* or *later on* differ from *early* or *later*? Doesn't *started up* mean the same thing as *started*? "But," you protest, "that's the way people talk." True, that is the way people talk. But what, pray tell, does naturalism have to do with the movies? The answer is almost nothing. The same is true for the *hello* and *good-bye* in telephone conversations and chance meetings. They should almost always be cut. Such "natural speech" is not informative, nor does it add anything to characterization or plot.

Another way to strike unnecessary chatter from your script is to remember that film characters do not partake in small talk. If your scene includes an apartment building doorman, your character will not stop to chat about the weather, the events of the day, or the health and well-being of the doorman's three rottweilers. In fact, the doorman will be addressed only if doing so advances the plot.

>CHARLIE
>You must give this package to Turner when he comes by.

or provides information or enhances characterization

>
> CHARLIE
> I'll be gone several days. But if anyone
> asks, tell 'em you haven't seen me.

You should not repeat someone's name in dialogue ad-infinitum.

>
> SAMMIE
> Did ya' get the stuff we asked for, Harry?

>
> FRAN
> Yeah, Harry, we depended on you.
> So let's have it.

>
> GEORGE
> Harry, I don't want to hear any excuses this
> time. I mean how many chances you think
> we're giving you?

>
> BILL
> You keep badgering Harry like that, he'll
> never remember the doughnuts. Right, Harry?

Introduce your character by name only when he first appears in your screenplay. While it might seem more dramatic at first, constantly referring to someone by their given name sounds awkward, strained, and artificial.

The A-B technique is a great first step to build dialogue, and dialogue surgery is a good second measure. But dialogue problems can (and often do) arise in spite of these practices. These are usually first draft snags and are easily corrected. (Easily corrected, that is, as long as you know what to seek and what to dismiss.) These impediments usually arise from what I consider the ten most common dialogue glitches. So another way to doctor your dialogue is to recognize the following ten errors:

1. Too Obvious: When you can show it, you do not need to say it. You describe a winter storm as a hard snow with drifts up to ten feet and wind blowing so fierce some hurricanes would be embarrassed. Cars are frozen to their spots, power lines are down and sparking, and even a sled dog would be hard put to find his way in such conditions. You lose points with endless chatter about, "Isn't this some storm?" or "Cold enough for you?" etc.

Unless there is something in your story that demands elucidation, let your visuals do the talking. Nothing is accomplished and much is lost by needless chatter.

2. Too Choppy: There was a character on Saturday Night Live who would base her entire routine on being confusing. She would tell a story in the following manner:

"I went into the, you know. And then I did. . .and I went over to the . . .and got to the. . .and did. . .then I left for. . .and went there to see . . .and made it from the. . .and had to be. . .where I saw. . ." etc.

Obviously, nothing about the story made sense, and for the sake of humor, it wasn't supposed to. Your characters, however, must be clearly understood — at least to the audience and to the other characters in your film. One incomprehensible character is bad enough, but a screenplay filled with them will result in consistent and well-deserved rejections.

3. Too Repetitious, Too Repetitious, Too Repetitious: Don't repeat the same sentence or idea — albeit in a slightly different way — over and over and over and over. If you have established that the job must be done by nine-o'clock, you do not need to say

> JOHN
> The man told me nine sharp. Not one
> minute past or it would be bad news for
> all of us.

And later

> SAMMIE
> Zero nine hundred has got to be it. Otherwise
> it'll be a mess none of us is gonna appreciate.

And some time later

> JUDE
> Nine o'clock sharp as a needle! Nothin'
> makes us gain a thing after nine.

And once more (just in case we missed it the other three times)

> CRAIN
> We have to be there at nine to run
> a line. If not, no dime.

The previous example may seem absurd, but I see this type of repetitive prattle in many of the scripts I read and critique. Say what you need to say only once, clearly and succinctly. Trust that you have done your job, and the audience will do theirs.

4. Tooooooooooooo long: We've been over this before, but it needs to be emphasized. Long speeches quickly become wearisome and few readers will remember them. Even if you feel a long speech is necessary, break it up visually on the page.

There are ways to make a long speech work. If, for instance, a candidate for public office is speaking, focus on the crowd or behind the stage. You might want to show a mysterious guy moving forward slowly, stealthily as if he is a threat to the speaker. If the speech is on radio or television, focus on how the listeners respond.

In *Network*, Howard Beal challenges his listeners to yell out that they are "mad as hell and aren't going to take this anymore." His long speech is broken up as the camera switches to the people in the booth, to Diana Christensen wanting to know if they were screaming it in Atlanta and Baton Rouge, to the reaction of a family watching the broadcast, and then to their neighbors' reaction. Beal's speech — broken by changing visuals, characters, and emphasis — is one of the most powerful speeches in all of filmdom.

5. Too Similar: Your script and characters will not be believable if all of your characters sound alike. If you listen closely, you will find that each person usually has a distinct speech pattern. Cadence, expressions, shorthand references, and voice modulation quickly identify one character from another. Studies of comics who do wonderful impersonations have shown that no matter how good the imitation, their voice patterns do not come close to matching the vocal patterns of the original.

How a character says something is significant. One of the best reasons for using A-B dialogue is to provide each character with both a unique voice and a reason for speaking.

6. Too stilted, artificial, or bookish: Sure, if one of your characters sounds like William F. Buckley, okay. But if they all sound like him, you will have about as many people attending your movie as watched *Firing Line* — actually, *Firing Line* might have had more. Even in academia, or in any scientific or intelligentsia community, there will be differing styles and expressions of speech.

7. Too Preachy: Dialogue in a filmscript exists to tell a compelling story. Messages, on the other hand, should be left to email and text messaging. Preaching, moralizing, or explaining the meaning of the action will negate the impact of your story. You create your plot and characters and visuals to guide your audience through a good, compelling tale. If the audience discovers the fantasy is nothing more than a vehicle for some opinion or lecture, they will tune out, turn off, or won't bother showing up.

Audiences find their own meanings and messages in movies, and sometimes do so in spite of the intentions of the writers, actors, directors, and others involved. A good film generates several interpretations — that is the nature of creative expression. The writer, the script, or the characters should not determine what the visuals and speech mean or should mean. The writer's duty is to entertain, period. And entertaining usually takes all the skill and talent one can muster. Accomplish this and the rest will take care of itself.

8. Too Introspective: The thoughts and emotions of a character should be shown and not told. Visual action expresses what a character believes and how a character changes. Some writers try to accomplish this through *Voice Over* (V.O.). I am not wild about this technique because it often interferes with the story by providing verbal exposition of what the audience has already seen and concluded for themselves. On the other hand, *Sunset Boulevard, Out of Africa*, part of *It's a Wonderful Life, Forrest Gump,* and *Million Dollar Baby* (to mention a few) use Voice Over as a tool to enhance the story and not as a substitute for the action.

A huge difference exists between the way introspection is portrayed in the above films and the way most writers portray introspection. Often, soliloquy is used as a substitute for the visual expression of a character's feelings. Soliloquy can be used successfully in a play or novel, but because it generally slows or halts the action in a film, I do not recommend that you use it in your screenplay. The personal revelation in your script or film can come during the *baring of the soul*, but even then, over-extended, inward speech can turn whiney and self-indulgent. It is better to reveal character through terrific visuals rather than with endless dialogue.

9. Too False: This occurs when an event in the story happens for no reason other than to move the plot along. You have probably seen and heard this in films a few too many times.

If a couple is arguing furiously over something, you can't just have one of them exclaim after a while, "Oh, honey, you're right, let's make up from this silly argument." Ending an argument for no other reason than you need to *move 'em up and head 'em out* is not enough. You need a transition or a logical sequence of dialogue to either end or soften the disagreement if that is where the story and characters are headed. Ending an argument for no good reason is no more rational than using plot devices for no good reason. You wouldn't have the good cops leave their star witness unprotected and vulnerable. Yet how many times have we seen just that?

If you allow your story to proceed to a deceptive conclusion, the only one who will be deceived is you.

10. Too Unbelievable (People just don't talk like that.): This category really contains all of the above, plus a little more. Once in a while, I'll read a script in which the dialogue sounds nothing like any human being I know, have known, or ever will know, would possibly say. And it is not just the alien from the bizarre planet Xerrmillo who speaks like no other, but every other character in the screenplay.

Dialogue must not be naturalistic, but it must be realistic. People use contractions, phrases, some slang, speech patterns, and shorthand to distinguish themselves from each other. Your audience needs to believe it is hearing real talk from real people.

One way of capturing the framework of speech is to use your listening skills — that is, well, eavesdrop. I am not for one second suggesting you bug someone's room or phone. I am suggesting that you listen to conversations without becoming a participant. Go to places where people gather, and simply listen. If you are writing about a certain type of place or atmosphere, attend as an observer and chronicler. Catch the conversations in line at the store, movie theater, or concert. When I lived in the Washington, D.C. area, I heard the most fascinating conversations on the yellow or blue line Pentagon routes. For instance, you would not believe the genius that went into inventing the $800 toilet seat. But hey, that's another story for some other time.

Does extended dialogue ever work? Yes, if your characters have fascinating things to say and fascinating ways of saying them. For instance, Quentin Tarantino's dialogue is lengthy and involved. But give the man his due. Most of his dialogue is excellent from start to finish.

According to one article I read, he used a book entitled *Figures of Speech-60 Ways to Turn a Phrase* by Arthur Quinn. I found the book academic but fascinating. It suggests distinct ways of fashioning and using the spoken word, and in that sense, is beneficial for anyone wanting to write film or fiction. While Tarantino may have used some of the ideas in the book, his style is his own. And just because his style works for him, it does not follow that it automatically works for any other screenwriter.

Certain styles created by one writer often become the rage until people realize that what that writer created is his or hers alone. When Shane Black's *Lethal Weapon* became the phenomenon, many writers tried to copy Black's talk-to-the-reader style. The style didn't become tiresome, but the writers did. The same holds true for Tarantino. Copying a style rarely succeeds. Create your own approach, your own phrasing, your own way of describing the action in the script and delivering the dialogue.

With dialogue, less is definitely more. Ask yourself, *Is this speech absolutely necessary?* or *Does this speech give information or enhance characterization that could be better shown?* If it doesn't, then delete it.

Dialogue can be a blessing or a curse, so pay attention to it! If you are stingy with the dialogue you include, and merciless with the dialogue you delete, you will be amazed at how much information and impact you can convey in just a few short, well-crafted speeches.

Chapter 16
Rhythm and Rhyme and Harmony

Harmony in a script is accomplished through parallels, connectives, pacing, ellipses, subplots and subtext.

There are many good scripts in existence that have never been bought, produced, or even considered. The problem is that they're good scripts, not great scripts. And the difference between the numerous good scripts and the truly special ones is that the special ones have a sense of rhythm, cadence, and harmony that balance and enhance them. This, in part, is attributed to the factors of *rhyming* and *connectives*, *pacing* and *ellipses*, and *subplots* and *subtext*.

All of these devices also deepen the content, empathy, and sense of movement in your script. Indeed these little things add up to a lot. So it's worth learning what they are and how to use them.

Rhyming and Connectives

Rhyming and *connectives* are story devices that use similarities to depict change. They help the audience — and even the characters — better understand their world, and they have been used in stories ever since stories have been told.

Pictographs from ancient Native American tribes in New Mexico, which have been interpreted as stories handed down by those tribes, show certain symbols constantly repeated. In a PBS documentary about these hieroglyphics, an interpreter explained that these repeated pictures helped ancient audiences remember their stories. Repeated phrases, too, have often been used to rhyme. How many times does Homer use the term, *rosy-fingered dawn*? And repeated actions are another form of rhyming. For instance, can you remember the numerous ways Miles imbibes his favorite beverage in *Sideways*?

Repetition is important in our own lives as well. Seasonal cycles such as the migration of birds flying north for the summer and south for the winter, yearly holidays, or for some, the opening of football or baseball season, create a cherished sense of familiarity.

When many of us were children, our parents or guardians recorded our growth on a wall or door. The changing marks indicated physical growth, and if we stop to think about it, mental and emotional growth as well. That, too, is *rhyming*.

Moving is a type of personal rhyming. One piece of advice that many give or get about moving to a new location is to take something with you to remind you of home. It is a rhyme and a connective that softens the trauma associated with change and helps you establish yourself in your new location.

Rhyming

Writers create rhyming scenes for two basic reasons. First, audiences, like individuals, vary in their tolerance to change. But change is what movies are all about. Just as the cycles of nature help us deal with real change, rhyming scenes help an audience accept changes in characters, setting, and/or situations. The second reason is to keep a lid on the budget — a topic I will discuss later in this section.

The writer has several types of rhyming devices at his disposal. Scenes that begin the same as other scenes in the film but end differently are rhyming scenes. Scenes that begin differently but end the same are also rhyming scenes. Scenes that take place in the same location, or scenes depicting similar circumstances or people also rhyme.

Remember the several meal scenes in *Kramer vs. Kramer*? One usually well-remembered scene is when Ted tries to fix French Toast for his son. He makes a mess of the toast, the meal, and the kitchen.

Another rhyming scene occurs when Ted and his son are eating dinner. Billy is acting up, and Ted tells him he can't have the ice cream he brought home for dessert. Billy leaves the table. Ted tells him not to go to the freezer. Billy goes to the freezer, grabs the dessert, and brings it back to the table. Ted tells Billy not to eat the ice cream. No points for guessing what the boy does next. The scene ends with Billy being punished and sent to bed. Some limits have indeed been set.

The last of these rhyming scenes involves Ted and Billy again fixing French Toast. This time, they both work together as a team. They make no mess, and they even try to have some fun as they mix the eggs and milk.

These scenes rhyme. They take place in the same location and with the same people, but the outcome is different in each case. They reveal character growth and make the audience comfortable with the changing relationship between Ted and his son.

Screenwriters help their audiences adapt to change by returning them to a setting or situation that they saw and accepted early in the film. Whether the rhymes are the training scenes for the bicycle races in *Breaking Away*, the boxing matches in *Million Dollar Baby*, the times Kay and Jay use their numerous and sometimes exotic weapons in *Men in Black*, or the interior scenes in *Return of the Secaucus Seven*, they each present us with something familiar and comforting while simultaneously forcing us to adapt to the changes in the characters.

In *Murphy's Romance*, Murphy takes Emma's son Jake on a trip in his early model car. Jake asks if the car will go any faster. Murphy says no, he is driving the car as fast as it will go. The boy is clearly disappointed. In the same scene, Murphy stops his car to give a ride to an older friend. After a brief time, the friend yells at Murphy to stop the car. The friend gets out quickly, complaining that Murphy always drives his car too darned fast.

One type of movie that is slightly more challenging to rhyme is the *road show*. In road shows, the main character is on a physical journey toward a goal or destination. These films are numerous and include *Easy Rider*, *Harry and Tonto*, and *Journey of Natty Gann*. Because it's difficult for characters to return to a specific setting in a road show film, the writer needs to create specific situations to help the audience accept the character shifts. Scenes of Natty riding with her wolf in railroad boxcars in *Journey of Natty Gann* are rhyming scenes. Harry's visits to his various relatives in *Harry and Tonto*, and the motorcycle scenes in *Easy Rider* rhyme as well.

In addition to comforting the audience, rhyming serves the essential purpose of holding down a film's cost. You already know that (with the exception of the occasional experimental film) movies are not shot in chronological sequence. The crew doesn't shoot one scene or shot, schlepp the entire operation across town for the next shot, and then return for whatever follows.

All scenes in one location are shot as close together as possible and then the crew schlepps the camera and equipment someplace else. Remember the show *Hee Haw* — don't be too quick to snicker, it stayed on the air for over twenty years. They could tape six months worth of shows in three-and-a-half weeks by using a modified version of rhyming scenes. The corn field jokes would all be done at the same time. One act (a singer or band) would perform, tell a few jokes, and leave to make room for the next act. The crew taped the sequences together and edited everything later. Rhyming saved the producers time and money and made possible what would otherwise have been a production nightmare.

Rhyming often appears naturally in your screenplay. Still, you need to recognize what it is and where it occurs in your script. If rhyming scenes are missing, you must purposely insert them; plant them in your scene cards and use them liberally in your story. Rhyming can keep an audience engaged in a scene even when change and discord are making them slightly (or significantly) uncomfortable.

Connectives

Connectives are similar to rhyming and involve the repeating of objects, images, or phrases at different places in the script to represent change and to give a sense of completeness to the story. Seeing or hearing these elements many times over the course of a movie, gives an audience the sense that the different settings and situations in the movie are connected and whole. In other words, even though the story may cover several days, weeks, months, years, etc. of film time, and even though the audience has only been sitting in the theater for an hour-and-a-half or two hours, they feel as if they've seen a whole, unified story, and that they, too, have experienced everything the characters have.

The birdhouse in *Witness* is a connective that takes on a unique symbolism. John Book knocks it down with his car when he first tries to leave the Amish community, and rebuilds it when he's living at the farm. He puts it back up just before he leaves the farm for the final time — and he and Rachel spend time together beneath it.

Another powerful connective from *Witness* is grain. The audience's eye focuses on it three times during the opening sequence. At Rachel's house after the funeral of her husband, the one food placed on the plates at the table is bread. Later in the script, Rachel hides the bullets from John's gun in a flour filled jar, and toward the end of the film, John kills one of the bad guys by burying him in corn kernels in a grain silo.

Connectives can be as obvious as the neuralyzer in *Men in Black* or the haunted wall mural in *Diva*. And let's not forget Forrest's box of chocolates and his numerous experiences with buses in *Forrest Gump*, and Harry's 44 magnum in the *Dirty Harry* series counts whether you're feeling lucky or not.

As for verbal connectives, Gatsby's "Old Sport" certainly qualifies;

Maggie calling Frankie "Boss" in *Million Dollar Baby* connects as well; so too does Rick Blain's "Here's looking at you, kid," in *Casablanca*.

As with rhyming, you must purposely place connectives into your script; place them in the first scene, or first act, or any new location crucial to the plot. By strategically placing your connectives at various points in your script, you connect the different parts of the work with objects or phrases already familiar to the audience.

One of my teachers suggested that you use a personal, physical connective to help inspire you as you write your script. That is, buy or find some object that represents what you're writing, and keep that object by your computer, typewriter, or pen and paper as you tackle your screenplay. Keep it there to remind yourself that what you're writing — from beginning to end — is connected to things that are important and meaningful to you.

Pacing

Sad films make some of us cry, slow films drive most of us up the proverbial wall. Remember that *pacing* and *movement* are as important to your script as they are to your film. As I discussed in Chapter 5 and more extensively in *Formatting Your Screenplay*, the look of the page — which indicates the pace of the film — is paramount (no pun intended) to the success of your script. Long, slow passages containing too much ink tend to be *dressed to kill* or perhaps *gone with the wind*. Crisply written pages containing short paragraphs of both direction and dialogue, all formatted correctly, will be the *secret of your success*.

In addition to good formatting, you'll need to employ other techniques to keep your script on pace. One of these techniques is to avoid grouping exposition, dialogue, or characterization. Another is to give your hero some O.S. (Off Screen) time. A third is to use ellipses, or time jumps, to drive the story forward.

Grouping, as you may have already surmised, is stuffing too much into too little. There is no need to give the audience your character's bio when you first introduce her. If she's a major character, you have 90 to 100 pages or more to provide some personal history. If your character isn't that important, your audience doesn't need to know that much about her.

Exposition grouping usually results in talking heads, or way more detail than anyone needs (or frankly wants) to know. Dialogue grouping — defined as greater than one-and-a-half pages of dialogue without some type of significant break for action or direction — will result in a tedious and slow screenplay. When you explain more than anyone wants to hear, even if something in your dialogue is vital, your audience will probably already have tuned out.

Insure good pacing by making sure your hero is never on-screen the entire time. Always switch to another setting, different characters, or other situations whenever you find your hero pursuing normal, everyday activities that do not advance the plot. One solution is to dive into a subplot. This gets your lead guy or gal off screen for a while and adds depth and intrigue to your main story.

Ellipses

Film time is not real time. The last movie you saw probably covered a period of days, months, years, or perhaps millennia. How long were you in the theater? (I'm not asking how long it felt like you were in the theater.) You were there probably less than two or two-and-a-half hours. One way to quickly jump your story forward is by using ellipses. *Ellipses* are those time jumps that allow you to compress real time and concentrate only on the moments essential to the story. If, for instance, you wanted to show a student leaving a classroom and meeting someone outside the school, do you want to record all of the real-life steps that student takes? If so, here's how the scene might look:

1. Rises from a desk
2. Maybe exchanges small talk with friends
3. Exits the room
4. Walks or runs down the hallway
5. Opens the doors to the outside
6. Steps outside
7. Greets a friend

The above sequence of events is mostly naturalistic. Nothing happens between events 1 and 7 to advance the story, and the audience can decipher and fill in everything that happens during those few moments anyway. A better way to relate the scene and keep your script moving at a dynamic pace is to start with event number one and jump — via a slug line — to event number seven.

Sometimes just a few seconds or minutes are skipped. Other times you bypass years or centuries. *Alice Doesn't Live Here Anymore* begins with a moment from the main character's childhood. Once concluded, the time-line jumps to that of the character as an adult. In *2001: A Space Odyssey*, in one neat match cut, a bone hurled into the air transforms into a space ship approaching the moon. We travel millions of years in a matter of seconds.

Obviously there are time periods between boxing matches in *Million Dollar Baby*, gaps in Howard Hughes' life not shown in *The Aviator*, time periods not relevant to the legal case in *Erin Brockovich*, but in each case the audience is capable of filling in the omitted period. Any important incidents that may have been excluded in the time jump can always be disclosed in exposition.

Ellipses keep you from writing material not pertinent to your story. They save space, time, and money, quickly advance the plot, and keep the narration focused on the key factors in your story. So if an incident or span of time is not pertinent to your plot, skip it and use ellipses as the key to keeping your script on pace and in the race.

Subplots

Subplots are those other stories in your script that are connected to and affect the outcome of the main plot. A film, because of its length, usually has no more than two or three subplots. Each subplot, while a part of the main story, is also a plot and story by itself. This means that each subplot has its own three-act structure and its own protagonist and antagonist.

When choosing the protagonists and antagonists for your subplots, be aware that you cannot have both the protagonist and antagonist of your main plot be the protagonist and antagonist of any one subplot. You may have one of these main characters as protagonist or antagonist of a subplot, but not both.

Another screenwriting feature to be aware of is the difference between the main plot and the "A" plot. The main plot is what the film is about, while the "A" plot is often the most compelling story in the film.

In *Witness*, the main plot is a murder mystery. But the film's most compelling story is the forbidden love affair between John Book and Rachel. This is the "A" plot, and it's what moves the story forward and maintains our interest throughout the movie.

The other subplots in *Witness* have to do with Rachel and her now tenuous position in the Amish community, and the relationship between John Book, his partner, and the police.

In *Sideways* the main story is about two friends who take a week off to visit the vineyards in California wine country to taste and learn about the wines produced there. The "A" plot centers on protagonist Miles and antagonist Maya and how Miles' life changes over the course of the week. The "B" plot concerns Jack and how his womanizing ways don't really change despite his upcoming wedding. And of course, the "C" plot focuses on the relationship between Miles and Jack.

The "A" plot, being the most important subplot — and sometimes the most significant part of the script — might consume six or more scenes. The "B" plot could use up four (or a few more), and the "C" plot might need three or more scenes to tell its story.

Subplots, then, constitute a substantial portion of your screenplay, and you need to spend as much time and energy on them as on your main plot.

As discussed above, in most films the main plot, the "A" plot, and the remaining subplots are connected by the same plot line, the same characters, and the same settings and circumstances. But there is a certain type of film in which the main story and the "A" story have completely separate functions. I call them *discovery tales*.

In a *discovery tale*, one or more of the characters learns something about themselves or their histories by hearing or experiencing someone else's story. Such films include *War of the Roses, Bridges of Madison County, Little Big Man, The Princess Bride*, and even *Million Dollar Baby*. In most of these films the central characters of the main story are really minor characters not involved, or only peripherally involved, in the "A" story.

In *War of the Roses'* main story, a lawyer influences his client by telling him about another client's divorce. The "A" story's protagonist and antagonist, though, are the couple in the story. *Bridges of Madison County's* main story centers on two grown children who discover an unknown part of their late mother's life. The "A" story's central characters are the mother and the photographer. In *Little Big Man's* main story, the interviewer comes away with a better understanding of the old west as well as of his own prejudices about cowboys and Indians. The "A" story's chief characters are Jack Crabb (the interviewee) and his Native American grandfather. In *The Princess Bride*, the main story revolves around the bond that develops between a grandfather and his grandson because of a story the grandfather reads. The "A" story's principal characters, however, are the swashbuckling hero Westley, his love Buttercup, and the evil Prince Humperdinck. And in *Million Dollar Baby*, Scrap is writing the entire story in a letter to Frankie's daughter, Katie.

There is no real rule concerning when to begin or end subplots. It is probably best to begin at least one subplot in the first act and the others early in the second act. (They should definitely all start before the mid-point of the second act.) It is always better to begin a subplot where it best falls in the story and to end it for the same reason. While subplots have their own structure, they must all dovetail with the characters and story of the main plot, and all subplots should be resolved by the end of the movie.

The only rules for subplots are

1. Never leave a subplot unfinished.

2. Always make sure the main plot and the "A" plot are clear and fill the majority of time and space in your script.

3. Do not include too many subplots. Having too many subplots usually means that the main plot and/or "A" plot will not be well enough defined, and the script simply will not work.

Subtext

One of my favorite examples of subtext is from *Annie Hall*. Alvin and Annie (remember all those teachers who told you to never begin your main characters' names with the same letter) talk after the tennis match. Of course, what they are saying has nothing to do with what they are *saying*. We know this because subtitles reflecting the characters' thoughts have been added for comic effect.

She thinks, *I'm making a fool out of myself in front of this guy.* And he thinks, *I wonder what she looks like naked.* The old courtship dance progresses full blown while the conversation between them remains cautious.

The *Annie Hall* scene is a perfect illustration of subtext. *Subtext* is what's really going on between or among characters, not what's happening on the surface. Subtext reveals the hidden meanings of conversations, actions, and decisions. It's what is truly in the minds and hearts of the characters.

Another wonderful example of subtext comes from *Tootsie*. When Michael is Tootsie, Julie tells her that she wants men to be more honest with her. She wants them to stop beating around the bush with phony lines and seduction techniques and just say, "I want to make love with you."

When Michael is again himself, he approaches Julie at a party and says, "I want to make love with you." Instantly, she throws a drink in his face.

As we discussed in Chapter 14, everything a character does in a scene relates directly to winning that scene. If she wins, it means that the other characters — who are also trying to win the scene — lose. This is conflict. This is two dogs, one bone. Your character's actions, body language, and dialogue all should be calculated toward achieving his goals in the scene. But the catch is that your character can't afford to reveal his real goal. For as soon as he tells someone else — as Michael did with Julie — it will be easier for that other character to prevent him from achieving it. The meaning of the words, and the intent of the action or body language is always found between the lines, beneath the surface, or hidden within some plan or ritual.

Revealing your subtext does nothing but turn a strong character into a weak character. As a writer, you need to be aware of the subtext in your script, but you must never allow your characters to reveal it — unless for a planned effect. Once you allow a character to telegraph his hidden thoughts, the other characters in the film will clearly have the advantage over him.

Rhyming and *connectives, pacing* and *ellipses, subplots,* and *subtext* are all devices that can enhance your script. Many of these will fall naturally into the stories and scripts you write. But you should always be aware of them and know when and how they can be used. The more aware you are of these small (but often overlooked) devices and how to use them, the better your chances of creating a winning script.

Chapter 17
First Things First

The first three pages introduce your entire script, and it's essential to make a great introduction.

I have talked with several readers (coverage editors) and each has told me in his own way that the first scene of the script generally determines whether they will even consider the work. One reader said, "If the first scene is terrific, I will continue reading even if the second scene isn't as good, as long as it picks up after that. But if the first scene isn't good, then I most likely will stop there."

First scenes — like first impressions — can determine the success or failure of your script. It makes no sense to work for months on your wonderful story if you crash at the opening.

Certainly, every scene in a script is important, but first scenes must shine. Why? Because they are what hook your audience into a story that must hold their interest and suspend their disbelief for the next two hours. An engrossing first scene, however, doesn't necessarily mean a slam-bang, blow-em-up Indiana Jones or James Bond type opening. Openings can be as gentle as the beginning of *Ordinary People*, as off-beat and darkly funny as *Men in Black*, as innocuous as *Sideways*, as seemingly safe as *Alien*, as humorous as *Airplane*, as action packed as *Million Dollar Baby*, or as terrifying as the attack exercise in *War Games*.

In seven pages or fewer, an opening scene must balance adroitness, speed, clarity, appeal, and emotion. It must transport us to a new place, introduce us to new characters, make us experience something fresh and engaging, and set up a believable, dynamic tale that will keep us enthralled from page one. Creating an excellent first scene is an amazing feat, but if you want a winner each time, you must perform that feat for every screenplay you write.

How can you be sure your first scene will succeed? There are about thirty elements that help make a strong first scene. If you know what these elements are, you can include them in your scene and ensure that they have accomplished their objective.

I have divided these elements into eight parts. The first two parts are concerned more with the *opening*, or the first two or three pages of your script. They are

Initial Considerations
Overture

The next six parts have to do with the first scene in general and will be covered in the next chapter.

Now let's examine these first two parts, and discover how and when to use their various elements.

Initial Considerations

Time
Location (place)
Genre
Major Character Introduction
Dialogue

Time and Location

The first two elements — *time* and *location* (place) — are always introduced in the primary slug. But remember, you're writing for a visual medium, so time and place must be conveyed to the theater audience as well. The process at this point becomes a bit more complicated, but, as with many complications, it also opens new opportunities for self-expression and creativity.

Say you begin your slug

EXT. NASHVILLE, TN - DAY   (WINTER 1951)

Okay, the reader knows it is winter 1951 in Nashville, but the direction paragraph or paragraphs that follow also must provide the *audience* with this information. So the following description might include cars and their 1951 license plate tags, the clothes people are wearing, the front page of a newspaper and/or a weathercast talking about possible snow in the next few days. At the opening of your script, the bridging in and set up can be somewhat more descriptive and novelistic than in the rest of the script. We will delve further into this in the *overture* section.

As discussed in Chapter 6, you should also include historical time in your first primary slug. In historical time, PRESENT means the time at which the crew begins shooting the film. Remember that the time between when your script is bought and the commencement of principle photography (the first day of shooting) will be a minimum of two years. So, if you use the current year as your historical time, it will become a period piece by the time the film goes into production.

Providing a date or time other than PRESENT — even if only a couple of years back — indicates that your work is a period piece. I have heard over and over (as you probably have) to never, positively ever write a period piece. In fact, an agent once dismissed a wonderful screenplay by one of my students because it was a period piece. So I looked up all the Academy Award winners for best picture since 1980. Out of twenty-five at this time, eighteen are period pieces. Go figure!

If your film is a historical piece or some futuristic fantasy, don't rely on graphics or titles to relate time and place. The filmmakers may add those, but it's still up to you to give the essential items their proper visual and/or verbal introduction.

One last word about time and location: Even if you open PRESENT in a familiar city like New York, Washington, D.C., or Los Angeles, you are still portraying *your* New York, *your* Washington, D.C., or *your* Los Angeles. The landmarks or neighborhoods you use, or do not use, to introduce the audience to your vision will depict a slightly or vastly different setting from the one audiences may know or think they know. In other words, each movie asks us to enter an alternate existence of some kind. At this stage, your audience is ready to accept this surrogate universe, but only if they see, feel, and emotionally connect with your world from the get-go. If they don't, they will get going all right, away from your work.

Genre

Is your script a mystery, space opera, action-adventure, drama, comedy, parody, western, thriller, horror film, or some other category? How do you convey this to your audience?

Sometimes the genre is crystal clear from the opening shots. In *Airplane*, the first image the audience sees is an airplane flying through an ocean of clouds with the plane's tail fin sticking just above that ocean. After a few seconds, the audience hears the theme music from the movie *Jaws*. At this point, I doubt anyone mistakes this movie for a serious drama or western.

In *Chinatown*, we quickly realize we are involved in a detective-drama. In *War Games*, the consequences of nuclear war haunt the film from the opening minutes. *Million Dollar Baby* is a sports film centered on boxing and the people who have the incredible mixture of determination, skill, and heart to compete in such an intense sport. *Men in Black* introduces us to aliens and ALIENS. *Forrest Gump* promptly settles into a life story after the fickle feather of fate, which we watch as it floats through the opening scene, lands upon our intrepid hero. We understand *Witness* to be a drama of culture clashes and personal sacrifice long before we agonize over the murder and its threatening consequences.

Imagine you are penning a romantic comedy. You might begin with a "date gone wrong" from one of the numerous TV dating shows. Or your dramatic script might open with a car passing or getting caught behind a funeral procession. On the other hand, your biographical film about a singer might show a concert hall, or for a film about an astronaut, you might choose a movie theater screening an outer space adventure.

Genre identification is critical for several reasons: First, it provides the audience with an infrastructure that enables them to quickly analyze this new world and its characters. It also allows the audience to presuppose the type of situations they will experience as the film progresses. Audiences will have different expectations for the characters and plot-line of an action-adventure film from what they'll have for a romantic comedy.

A third reason for specifying genre has to do with anticipating the ending. A specific genre suggests certain plausible endings. In a murder mystery, the audience will ultimately know *who done it* or how the guilty party gets caught or gets away. In an action-adventure romp or space opera, the audience expects the hero to win — or at least survive. In a drama, the audience presumes it will experience the ennobling of the human spirit. And in romantic comedy, the audience is certain that two people will somehow fall in love. Audiences take comfort in knowing how the story will end. What they pay and stay for is to discover how the characters achieve that ending.

Major Character Introduction

You need to introduce your protagonist or antagonist in the first few pages. Both may be presented, but at least one must be in the scene. As discussed in Chapter 3, characters can be present in a scene in myriad ways. Let's review.

Being physically present is the easiest and most common way of introducing a character, but it certainly isn't the only way. You can introduce a character by talking about her, or depict a character by having some object in the scene represent her or something she owns or identifies with. You may introduce a character by showing film or tape of her within your own movie. In *War Games*, we see a movie of Dr. Falken even though we believe he is dead. Also, showing the spirit or supernatural form of a character means there is more than a ghost of a chance that she has made the audience's acquaintance.

Openings where neither the protagonist nor antagonist are physically present are rare but can give the audience a better idea of how future circumstances will affect the protagonist. In *Shakespeare In Love*, we are introduced to Henslowe, the owner of the Rose Theater, as well as to Mr. Fennyman and his henchmen. Though Shakespeare is mentioned, the fact that the Rose must produce a play within the next three weeks is a crucial timetable to everything that transpires throughout the rest of the film.

Dialogue

Should you use dialogue on the first page? I have talked to several agents and producers and found that some say yes and others say no. What's a poor writer to do? (We assume the rich ones have already resolved this conundrum.) The answer seems to be to use dialogue on the first page only if it is absolutely needed.

I personally favor not using dialogue on the first page because audiences (even good, attentive audiences) can absorb only so much exposition at any one time. Throwing too much at an audience, especially at the beginning, will confuse them, or else something meaningful to the film will be lost or simply forgotten. After talking with friends and trying to gauge audience reactions when they see a movie in a theater, I have concluded that there are three factors that, taken together, seem to max out the attention spans of most moviegoers.

First, we are being subjected (willingly I admit) to a new time, place, and situation. Second, we are meeting and assessing new people we want to care about and new situations we want to understand. Third, the credits are usually rolling, letting the audience know who the actors are, and who directed, produced, distributed, and most significantly, *wrote* what the audience has paid good money to see. These three components are more than enough for any audience to handle. Adding dialogue at this point means that the audience must attune to one more element. And in my humble opinion that is simply one too many.

Okay, you think, *if I include dialogue, the audience probably loses the credits. Most times they pay little or no attention to them anyway.* Your reasoning is sound, but. . .for an infinitesimal nano-second don't you want those good folks to gaze up at that wondrous silver mesh and read your name as the screenwriter, even if an infinitesimal nano-second later they treat you like my agent treats me and forget your very existence?

Inserting dialogue means my name is removed from the audience's reference, completely ignored. I don't even get a fifteenth of a second of fame. No thrill of victory, only the agony of delete.

Now, as promised, let's discuss the all-important overture.

Overture

Themes

Much like musical theater where the audience is presented with a collage of the tunes and songs they will experience during the course of an evening, a cinematic overture acquaints the audience with the themes, rhythms, plights, and predicaments that will occupy their time and attention over the next couple of hours.

A film *overture* expresses visually (and sometimes verbally) the themes and subject of the movie. In *Witness*, Peter Weir's brilliant direction takes us across a wind-blown field of grain. Then we see a line of people, all dressed as if they were from the eighteenth century, following a horse-drawn hearse. Later, we attend a service for the deceased. Then we're shown farmers harvesting hay bales. We see the family of the deceased riding in a horse and buggy. And finally, we view a modern concrete highway with a truck forced to travel at a slow crawl because it's behind that horse and buggy.

With only a very few words spoken, all the themes of the movie have been suggested. 'How,' you ask? Let's examine the images. The principal themes of *Witness* are land, nature, community, love, death, and culture clash. And all of these occur in the overture. Land and nature materialize in the first shots of the wheat field. (And as discussed earlier, wheat or grain becomes a prominent connective throughout the movie.) Community and love are clearly depicted by the people, their actions, and the clothes they wear. The theme of death is obvious from the funeral. And the clash of cultures is depicted by the huge semi, a giant behemoth that must give way to an ancient form of transportation.

A sense of foreboding, a foreshadowing of disorder and danger, is also vividly displayed in Weir's overture. As we traverse the wheat-blown field, light shadows formed by the blowing wheat move ominously across the landscape and provide a figurative warning of impending conflict.

Another visual (in a somewhat more obvious overture) transpires in *Back to the Future*. Clocks, clocks, o'clocks, and even more clocks fill the earliest shots. A contraption of metal arms and levers opens a can of dog food and delivers the food to a bowl heaped with more uneaten dog food. A laboratory filled with junk and discarded experimental contraptions soon appears. The news on the radio and television informs us of the year and also that the plutonium supposedly stolen from a nearby nuclear plant was simply misplaced. Next, a young man (whose face is not shown) powers up a huge stereo speaker and then blasts it on with an overpowering jolt. The blast propels the young man backward across the room, bouncing him into an easy chair, which crashes against a make-shift bookcase along the back wall.

Time is the first and main theme in *Back to the Future*. Also introduced are the mad but creative scientist, his friend and protegé, haywire experiments, and situations that are not what they first appear to be. The young man (Marty) who is zapped across the room, has taken only his first trip backwards. By this point, the basic themes of the movie have been shown clearly, succinctly, visually, and with very little dialogue.

Another excellent example of an effective overture comes from *Silence of the Lambs*. We open with Clarice running the obstacle course at the FBI Headquarters in Virginia. The day is foggy and slightly dark, and in tackling this course, we get the feeling that Clarice is either running toward or away from something terrifying.

Clarice is stopped by an FBI superior who tells her that Crawford — the head of Behavioral Sciences Service — wants to see her. As she leaves the obstacle course, she passes a sign with the following message: *Hurt, Agony, Pain, Love It*.

On the way to Crawford's office, she passes her roommate as well as several academy cadets cleaning their weapons. Then she steps into an elevator with a bunch of men, all of whom tower over her, which gives us an idea of what she's up against in her FBI training and what she might later face as an agent. Finally, she goes into Crawford's office.

In the office, she studies photos and articles about a serial killer labeled "Buffalo Bill" because he skins his victims. After some talk with Crawford (where we find out a little about Clarice) he assigns her with the "interesting errand" of interviewing the most notorious serial killer now in custody, Dr. Hannibal "the cannibal" Lecter.

Time and location are obvious from the beginning, not simply because a title tells us where we are, but because of the FBI logo on the man's cap. The foggy, dark woods and the way Clarice is attacking the obstacle course shows us that this is a serious drama, and the sign post with the *Hurt, Agony, Pain, Love it* message plays as both a reminder of the FBI training and an ironic statement of what's to come.

The scene where agents are cleaning their weapons at the FBI Headquarters is an obvious clue. And the introduction of Buffalo Bill and Hannibal Lecter set up the rest of the fantastic script.

The above examples lean toward an absence of dialogue on page one. Now let's study a film where dialogue occurs before any images appear on the screen. *Million Dollar Baby* begins with Scrap's Voice Over (V.O.). As the picture appears, we are taken to the middle of a boxing match where the focus is on Frankie Dunn, our protagonist. We find out a little something about Frankie's history and character through Scrap's narration, the film's visuals, and the description in the script itself — which is clearly relayed by the visuals. We also learn that boxing is a tough, dangerous sport and that a boxer must have skill, tenacity, and heart to stay in the game. Then we are quickly introduced to Maggie, her grit and personality and — even from the few lines she and Frankie exchange — surmise that these two will interact a lot more during the course of the film.

So what is *Million Dollar Baby* about? Certainly it's about boxing and the qualities a fighter must have to even step into the ring. But it's also a film about relationships, the trust a boxer has in her trainer and manager, and about the true meaning of family and friendship. The thrills and danger of boxing are evident from the outset. And with Scrap's V.O. discussing himself and Frankie, along with Maggie's introduction, the motif of friendship and family is hinted at as well.

Because the overture introduces the entire script, it gives the writer a bit more space to lure the audience into unfamiliar territory. The writer has enough leeway in the opening two or three pages to be somewhat more poetic, descriptive, and/or novelistic than at any other place in the screenplay. This does not imply a license to over describe, over-write, or over-use the language, just to overture with some of the best narration a writer can produce.

Foreshadowing

Foreshadowing literally means to indicate or suggest beforehand. In your screenplay, foreshadowing is a sign of things going amiss, of plans — especially the protagonist's — going awry. It lets the reader know that all will not stay predictable and obvious and that change, shifts, and surprises are on the way. The signs of foreshadowing do not have to be overwhelming, and in fact, many times they are quiet and subtle.

In *Men in Black*, the insect avoids being hit by various vehicles, then splatters against the windshield of a van. In *Sideways*, Miles' hangover and his lying about why he's late suggest more important consequences down (or up) the road. In *The Sixth Sense*, Dr. Crowe's wife Anna's breath forms beads of cold air, and she feels uncomfortable in her own wine cellar. And in *Erin Brockovich*, Erin not only doesn't get the job, she gets a parking ticket and breaks a nail.

In a sense, the overture is a bridging in for the script; it sets the tone, pace, and style of writing the reader will encounter. I cannot emphasize enough the importance of the overture to the beginning, and indeed, the entire screenplay. Present your new world, characters, and situations in an intriguing and engaging way, and you are well on your way to creating a produceable and saleable work.

Chapter 18
First Things First: The Sequel

Grab your reader by beginning a new journey for both reader and protagonist.

Once you move past the overture, you must pull your reader more deeply into your story. These next six sections emphasize the elements you will need to keep your reader and audience involved. They are

Attitudes
Page Pattern
Scene Elements
First Scene Reversal
People Who Need People
Future Considerations

Attitudes

Author's Attitude

The first attitude you must clearly communicate is your own. Be passionate about what you write. This does not mean in any way, shape, or form that you have a license to preach or send a message. As I said before, leave messages to e-mail. But you should be passionate about your story. You must want to tell your tale and believe that others will want to see and hear it. And that passion, that desire, must find its way onto the page without preaching or sermonizing.

If your vision and passion are missing, so too are the very emotions needed to carry your screenplay. One of the reasons a producer will buy your script is to purchase the unique voice you bring to the work. Ideas, thousands of them, float out there for everyone to grab. The techniques that shape those ideas into a story are what make one script hot and another not.

Main Character's Attitude

The main character's attitude plays as big a role in sculpting your script as the author's attitude. The main character does not need to have (or will even be presumed to have) the same beliefs as the author. One of the biggest misconceptions I hear is from people who attribute a quote from a character to what the writer believes. For instance, people say Shakespeare said, "Neither a borrower nor a lender be." Actually, we don't know what Shakespeare said or believed. We just know what his characters said and believed.

Attitude is derived strictly from a particular character. That character has personality traits that can differ from, or be similar to, the person who created her.

Sometimes you can have fun, and create great situations and characters by conceiving a main character who possesses values opposite from your own. The classic television sitcom, *All in the Family*, demonstrates how this "opposites attract" scenario enhances a story or idea. Norman Lear, the founder of one of the most progressive political organizations in the country, created Archie Bunker, one of the most memorable politically-incorrect characters in television history. This is a good example of opposing attitudes combining to create excellent storytelling.

Community Attitude

The third attitude is that of the community at large. Community standards or views have an impact on how we judge a person. Those views, in turn, can affect the character and how that character is judged by an audience. And since in the first scene we open with "normal," the community attitude and how it affects our hero is usually immediately important.

Community attitudes may also differ from that of the author or the main character. In another classic TV sitcom, *Family Ties*, much of the humor was derived from the conflict that resulted from Alex's conservatism, his parent's liberalism and his sisters' apolitical world views. It helps readers and audiences alike to perceive from the beginning what the various community belief systems are, how they relate, and what influence they have on characters and plot.

Page Pattern

Page pattern focuses primarily on correct formatting. I wrote *Formatting Your Screenplay* because I believe correct formatting is critical. But as important as good format is to your script as a whole, it's probably most important in the first scene. Page pattern also includes pacing, ellipses, idea balance, and placement.

Pacing

Pacing is concerned with mastering the rhythms of the screenplay; it involves blending writing and format style into a page arrangement that enhances the story you depict with your words.

A page heavy with ink, long, rambling description, and infinite talking-heads will not be taken seriously. But even a script with short descriptive paragraphs and succinct dialogue will be dismissed if the pages stray from the most intriguing action of the narrative. So pacing cultivates content as much as style, and a writer must convey both equally well.

Managing pace at the beginning can be tricky. The writer, given greater license to compose the overture, must be especially attuned to even the least amount of stagnation. It's too easy to stop and admire the roses, particularly if you've painted them so magnificently. Like everything in a film script, a little goes a long way. Your set-up may linger slightly, but too many details, too much prose, or too much symbolism will topple your story as readily as fatuous format will.

Once more, a hint of atmosphere is better than endless particulars. Make sure that your overture reinforces and promotes your story. Don't lose yourself or your reader in pristine prose that wanders aimlessly. Write your set-up with the idea that the first scene is still just a scene. It must, at minimum, fulfill every requirement specified for all scenes in your screenplay.

Ellipses

Ellipses, or time jumps, help you hit the highlights of your story in a timely manner. Ellipses target the places in a scene that advance your story and move smoothly to them, allowing you to emphsize those points without wasting momentum on marginal or naturalistic action.

Ellipses encompass the time you skipped. They can occupy a few minutes, days, weeks, months, or longer. But you need to introduce some sort of ellipses within the first scene — preferably within the first few pages. Why? Because each time an audience sees a film, they must be quickly reintroduced to some basic film conventions. One of these conventions is film time. Film time, which can occupy days, months, years, or more, still only requires 90 to 120 minutes of our time to sit and watch. Introducing this concept by including one or two time jumps early, quickly reinforces this particular film protocol.

Idea Balance

Another way to enhance the pacing of your script is to avoid bunching. Avoid drowning your audience with exposition, characterization, or even dialogue. The problem — especially in Scene 1 — occurs when the writer believes she must tell more than anyone needs or cares to know. Save the unessential explanations for later, or better yet, never.

Placement

Since a first scene balances overture and story, it makes idea placement moderately more difficult. Let me explain. One of the lessons my teacher at USC taught me was that most coverage editors learn to scan a script as opposed to reading every word. By scanning the script, the reader only catches what is easily seen on the page.

In other words, don't write some critical idea or clue or action at the bottom right of the page or even at any of the margins. Place it at or near the middle, and in the middle-middle if at all possible.

How then, do you place something indispensable in the middle of the page when pretty much everything at this point seems essential? The writer should determine the crucial elements and place them in the sight spots on the page. Everything may not be absorbed, but the reader should see the prime elements.

Scene Elements

Contact Point

In Chapter 12, we focused on how special the bridging-in or contact point is. The other scene elements must be handled with specialized care as well.

Conflict

Conflict must arrive by page two and preferably before. Any hint of tension between or among the characters, or even parenthetical to the action on screen, will help insert that note of conflict. It can be anything that portends future trouble, whether it be the struggle of opposing forces in *Terminator*, Henslowe's feet literally being held to the fire in *Shakespeare In Love*, or Howard Hughes' mother warning young Howard that he's not safe in *The Aviator*. Conflict can be anything that gives audiences that indispensable ingredient that connects them to the stories they read, see, and hear.

Let me give you an example how you might change an opening when the conflict just isn't there. One evening in class, a woman read the opening of her script, which went on for two-plus pages, portraying a perfect Christmas setting in a snow-covered suburban neighborhood replete with decorated trees, colorful lights, bright green wreaths, perfectly formed snowmen, and elegant yard displays. I finally asked, "What kind of film is this?" "It's a murder mystery," she said. "Oh. Then perhaps there should be a decapitated snowman," I suggested, "or someone could have sprayed the message, RIP, on someone's outdoor wreath." The hint of foreshadowing and conflict can be on the edge of the shot or scene, but there must be something in it that indicates that things are not necessarily as tranquil as they may seem.

Characterization

When you introduce your protagonist and/or antagonist, do you provide the audience with background information, traits, or insight that will help them distinguish that character from the others in your story? Of course you do. But as with everything in movies, a little is a lot, so give a little and let it make you a lot.

An overabundance of information will also kill your opening. For some inexplicable reason, writers think a reader or audience needs to know everything by page five. Actually, the opposite is true. Most information in the first scene comes from the *Initial Considerations* we detailed in the last chapter and the images composed in your work. Divulge histories slowly. Conceal puzzles or riddles — at least for a while — and avoid talking-heads at all costs.

Audiences, believe it or not, often appreciate discovering information and meaning on their own. We want to be able to say to ourselves, 'Oh, I get it. That's why he didn't tell the police about the mysterious pendant.' We enjoy it when characters and solutions are revealed slowly. As I've said before, if you show the shark at the beginning of *Jaws*, everyone gets up, goes home, and probably won't recommend the picture to friends. Characterization and exposition, like seasoning in a good meal, must be sprinkled in slowly, not dumped in a lump. Always hold something back. Finish each scene with the audience wanting to know more, see more, discover more, and question more.

Emotion

Regardless of how well you write, nothing works unless the audience reacts to it. Emotion has to exist in every scene, preferably on every page of every scene. Especially in the first few pages, something must trigger an emotional reaction, and the audience must continue to respond after that. So make sure that your pages convey laughter, hate, envy, anger, sadness, joy, nostalgia, or any of the thousands of emotions we humans can feel. If the first pages render no emotion, they will render nothing else.

First Scene Reversal

As discussed in Chapter 12, the first scene reversal is one of the key points in the entire script. Make sure to reveal your protagonist's normal life — or the events that will change your protagonist's normal life — before you pull the rug out from under him. It's this change that your audience wants to see, and it is absolutely necessary if you want the rest of your story to work.

People Who Need People

People

People who need people may or may not be the luckiest people in the world, but they *are* the people who must inhabit your film script even in the first scene. One of your main characters— protagonist or antagonist — must be introduced in the first scene. And at least one of your main characters — protagonist, antagonist, or both — must be introduced in the first scene.

Screenplays, after all, are not about non-organic species or landscapes. Moon rocks, unless anthropomorphized, probably won't make an especially exciting script topic. Even if their presence causes solar system-wide cataclysmic consequences, unless living, breathing, sentient beings are affected, who's gonna' care?

Others

Okay, so you agree the script needs a character. But just one character isn't going to grab a whole lot of folks. Screenplays about hermits are not inherently appealing. Writing alone in a cabin in the woods may be exactly what you need to create your story and style, but ultimately, someone else must read and react to your work.

I bring this up to make a simple point: You must have at least one person interacting with another person in the first pages of your script. If clothes make the person, people make the script.

Planning Ahead

Rhyming and Connectives

President Clinton's first campaign theme, *Don't Stop Thinking About*

Tomorrow, is also good advice for a screenwriter. You must use several staples to prepare your audience for the upcoming events in your story.

One staple is remembering to fasten your acts together. Be sure to plant at least one incident, location, or action in your opening scene that you will later use to rhyme or connect.

Destiny and Foreshadowing

In screenplays, the future is not just around the corner, it's smack dab right in front of you from the first slug. Change happens quickly. Events veer markedly toward the unexpected from the first scene reversal onward. Use some type of foreshadowing to let your audience know that change and trouble are on the way. A bumper sticker I see says, *My karma ran over my dogma*. Keep that in mind when crafting your screenplay.

The Next Scene

Realize, also, that some twenty-plus scenes will follow the first one. And no matter how brilliant your first pages, they are simply a set-up for the next segment. And that next segment a set-up for the next, and so on until the sequel. Each scene leads to something else. Don't box yourself in with a plot stopper like killing off your main character or suddenly causing all of your characters to disappear. It might make for an incredibly spectacular scene, but where do you go from there? Like a good chess player, always plan several moves ahead. And like a good screenwriter, be sure to use that scene card outline you created before you begin to write your screenplay.

One other note about planning ahead: Don't psych yourself out by page 5 or 6. I have seen writers who created spectacular first scenes but were never able to write the rest of the scenes in the script. Yes, write the best opening scene you can, but try not to let your initial success frighten you into believing that you can't do better. You've got a story to tell and the passion to tell it. Keep at it. Keep creating. Keep writing! And if you have a person or critique group you trust, follow their advice. They may not, at first, get you to where you want to be, but they might start you moving again in the right direction.

Character Arc

Have you given your characters an arc? No, not a boat with animals, but a general plan for how your protagonist and others might change over the course of your story. No one in real life, or in movies, changes in a straight progression. It's always several steps ahead, some to the side, one back, and then a few more forward. Where do you want your character or characters to be at the end of the movie? What do you want them to do, to think, to accomplish in the finale?

Character Facades

Once you have this character arc prepared, have you also added character facades that will be different by the final frames? That is, will your characters' clothes, speech patterns, life style, or some other outward expression of inward change be evident at the end of the story? This type of exterior evolution helps depict inner character transitions and gives audiences a clearer notion of how and why those adjustments occur.

A-B Dialogue

Introduce your audience to film time and film characters and also to film-speak. That is, when you initiate dialogue, make sure the A-B nature of it is clear and sharp from line one. This promotes the dissonance and conflict necessary to carry your screenplay to the very end. Film-speak in your opening helps readers adjust to the verbal exchanges that occur in your screenplay.

Energy

Have you maintained your passion? Don't let even one page of your screenplay lack the energy and devotion you hold for your ideas and work. A screenplay is like a long relationship. If you don't absolutely love it from the beginning, imagine how you'll feel about it by the umpteenth draft. Write what you love, your bliss. When you finish, sending your manuscript off in the mail will feel like the start of a well-earned vacation instead of a bitter, unplanned divorce.

Finale

Finally, you need to create a sense of ending. Of course, the audience won't know and shouldn't be able to guess the details, but they have to believe the story is headed toward a conclusion. I know you're thinking, 'Casablanca didn't have an ending until the final day of shooting.' Actually, the writers provided two separate endings and the director decided which one to use at the last minute. Nevertheless, inquiring minds want to know. What do they want to know? They want to know that

They will not starve to death before the final credits roll.
They won't have to pay the babysitter a fortune in overtime.
They will get home in time to see Saturday Night Live.
They will get home in time to see their children graduate.

A sense of ending, even from the moment the light casts upon the silver screen, reassures an audience that their night's entertainment will not last as long as the Michael Jackson trial.

In Chapters 17 and 18, we discussed a long list of elements. Many are similar, many overlap, many are contained in other chapters, and many complement one another. Learn each one well, what it does, and how it strengthens the opening scene. I promise this will make your opening scene stronger, more vibrant, and much more enticing.

I'm ending this chapter with a simple list of elements. Use this list to check how your first scene is progressing. Never forget that your first scene is the cornerstone of your script. You want one that will endure despite hurricane, flood, earthquake or the whims of the gods or Hollywood.

First Scene Requirements

I Initial Considerations
A. Time
B. Location
C. Genre
D. Major Character Introduction
E. Dialogue

II Overture
A. Themes
B. Foreshadowing

III The Attitudes
A. Author's Attitude
B. Character's Attitude
C. Community Attitude

IV Page Pattern
A. Pacing
B. Ellipses
C. Direction Balance
D. Idea Balance
E. Placement

V Special Requirements for Scene Elements
A. Contact Point
B. Conflict

C. Characterization
D. Emotion

VI First Scene Reversal
A. Begins Protagonist Change
B. Alters Protagonist's Course

VII People Who Need People
A. People
B. Others
C. Interaction

VIII Future Considerations
A. Rhyming and Connectives
B. Destiny and Foreshadowing
C. The Next Scene
D. Character Arc
E. Character Facades
F. Energy
G. Finale

Chapter 19
Information, Education, and Stepping Stones

There are many things you can do to get you and your script ready for the marketplace.

One story I sometimes hear when I begin a new class is about a well-known writer whose opening speech at a writers' conference admonished the students for not being at home writing. What absolute, arrogant crud.

Like other professionals, most writers can use mentoring or help. No one expects sports stars to perform well without years of training by one or more professional coaches. Tom Brady did not win multiple Super Bowls by staying home and throwing footballs through a tire.

Tennis players have coaches. Chess players have coaches. Many people in the business world constantly attend seminars and classes. Brain surgeons (we hope) have years of education and training. And most of today's great filmmakers had someone, or several someones, who not only showed them the ropes but may have helped them cut through the Gordian knot those ropes sometimes make. Don't writers deserve the same advantages?

Opportunities do exist. In fact, there are an amazing number of resources available to the aspiring (as well as the accomplished) screenwriter. The list includes

Books, Magazines, Newsletters
Classes, Workshops, Schools, and Conferences
Critique Services, Fee Readers
Critique Groups
Contests

One note: This chapter does not attempt to assess all or any of the individuals, organizations, or companies available to film and television writers. (There are too many, and the industry changes too quickly to try to list them in this book.) It simply provides a general category of services and suggests how to evaluate them.

Books, Magazines, Newsletters

Since the 1980s, the number of books about screenwriting has proliferated. In 1980, you could find a few. Today, it seems that number is either uncountable or equal to the number of pollutants hovering in the Los Angeles air, whichever is greater.

What should we read, and most importantly, what should we buy? I have included a list of my favorite books in an appendix at the back of this book. They are not necessarily the best books for everyone, but they have been helpful to me and my students.

How do you find the best books for you? First, ask yourself three questions: *What do I want to learn? What do I need to learn? What can I afford to buy?*

Most screenwriting books offer a much more theory-oriented, theater-influenced, or character-driven approach than I prefer. But even in those books, I have usually been able to find certain theories and techniques that have helped me with my own writing and teaching. However, you may favor one approach over another, so it's best to first survey before you buy.

Your library is a good place to start. Don't forget that if the library doesn't carry a particular title, you can usually order it through Interlibrary Loan. You can also visit your local independent bookstore. Oftentimes, they will be most willing to help you locate the right books as well as books that might appeal to you. You can also take advantage of the new, big bookstores, which are open fairly late and offer comfortable chairs and tables for your reading pleasure. In some cities there are bookstores just for the performing arts. These stores carry a far larger and better selection of screenwriting and film material than the normal, run-of-the-mill corporate book emporium.

You might also survey screenwriting magazines. These magazines — which you can find at bookstores, and sometimes at drug stores, supermarkets, and newsstands — offer valuable ideas and information about screenplay writing and marketing. They often review and advertise screenwriting books and newsletters and sometimes report on or advertise film schools and screenwriting seminars. They're a good way to discover what's out there and what might work for you.

Classes, Workshops, Schools, and Conferences

Like screenwriting books and magazines, the number of classes, workshops, and conferences has proliferated over the last two-and-a-half decades. And which ones you choose can have an effect on your writing career.

Weekend conferences and seminars can give you a good, general overview of how to produce and market your script, particularly if there's a good teacher or a few good panels available.

Other ways to find good conferences or weekend workshops are to talk to people who have been to them. Get on the screenwriting chat lines and listen, I mean read, as people discuss the various teachers, conferences, classes, schools, and on-line services that offer screenwriting courses.

Of course, weekend conferences can also have a downside. After all, a weekend leaves time for just an overview, and learning from a short lecture in a room with hundreds of other people is usually not enough to get you where you need to be. Also, some weekend seminars and conferences are quite expensive, and while one or two may be worthwhile, others do nothing but throw away your hard-earned dollars. You'll hear pretty much the same material at a couple of hundred-dollar weekend conferences as you will at a conference costing many hundreds of dollars. So paying those extra Benjamins for a panoramic view or a big name star or two is probably not in your best interest.

One perk many screenwriting conferences offer is the opportunity to "pitch" your screenplay to an agent or producer. This basically means the chance to verbally sell your script to someone who supposedly can say "yes" to a project. Learning and practicing pitching is one of the most valuable skills any writer can acquire, and something most writers will have to do constantly in their careers.

The main complaint I've heard about conference pitching is that sometimes the producers and agents who attend these workshops aren't really looking for new material or, if producers, lack the influence in their company to really greenlight a script. While getting the opportunity to practice your pitching skills can be a valuable experience, thinking that there is a chance to actually sell your script at one of these conferences may be, at best, a disappointment.

Another way to improve your screenwriting is to seek out a good, proven screenwriting teacher. But how do you find one? Chat lines or e-bulletin boards are good places to start. Sometimes your local or state film commission can be helpful, and if there's a screenwriting organization nearby, they should be able to provide you with valuable information about upcoming classes and events.

Remember that your local colleges may offer classes in screenwriting which can cost less and provide more in-depth information than a conference can. While this greater commitment can be a problem for some, it can also be a huge advantage. In my classes, we have time to read and critique scenes from student's scripts. The marked improvement you will see in your script will more than compensate for the cost and time of a semester-long course.

Obviously, not every instructor who teaches a screenwriting class is a good one. Even with recommendations, you will still need to do some homework. One of the most important ways to assess a screenwriting teacher is to look for credentials.

What do I mean by credentials? Some might look at whether a teacher has sold a script or a number of scripts. These are impressive achievements, and while it's good for a teacher to have a number of script sells to her credit, it's far better for you if her *students* have been successful. After all, you're not paying her to write a script for you, you're paying her to teach you how to create a winning screenplay.

Another way to assess a teacher is to talk to him before you enroll. Also, talk to students who have taken his class. Most schools have students fill out end-of-semester instructor evaluations. Sometimes the school will allow you to see these evaluations, and other times they may even appear on the internet. Reading them can be extremely helpful when deciding whether or not to take a particular class.

What is of utmost importance is that you learn to craft a script that is professional in every sense of the word. A good instructor, no matter where you find him, can help in this first, critical step toward selling your screenplay.

Critique Services, Fee Readers

There comes a time in most of our writing lives when friends, critique groups, teachers, or writing colleagues are unable to devote the time and effort necessary to help us hone the final draft of our script. So we search for a specialist to read, critique, edit, and assist us in perfecting our product.

This is the situation where a lot of screenwriters think about hiring an expert. There are many alleged experts out there, and every one of them is more than willing to take your money. But what you want is someone who knows how to critique screenplays, write a clear, knowledgeable analysis, make useful suggestions, and care about her work as much as you care about yours. The challenge is in finding the right person.

In *Formatting Your Screenplay*, I discussed the advantages of hiring an editor. A good editor is invaluable and can help you make your writing sharper, clearer, and more professional. But most prose editors don't have enough knowledge of scriptwriting structure to be of much help concerning story and content. The two types of experts who offer the most comprehensive help to the screenwriter are *critique services* and *fee readers*.

Several screenwriting organizations that offer critique services have appeared over the last few years. Some of these organizations sell their services for a very low fee. They also promise that after each script is diagnosed, it will be reviewed by a well-known, prestigious screenwriter.

Nothing seems wrong with this, and many times nothing is. But as a potential client, I would have some questions I would want answered before I spend my hard earned money — questions such as *who is reading this* and *what are his qualifications?*

If you would rather deal with a fee reader, there are some good ones who will critique your script. These readers are generally screenwriting teachers, analysts, or writers. And the good ones cannot only tell you if your script is good, bad, or ugly, but what measures you should take to improve your work. Fee readers probably will cost more because they tend to give your script closer scrutiny and the critique more attention. But before writing a check or giving out those magical sixteen credit card digits, you should find out as much as you can about any group or critic. Find out

— *how much they charge (including all hidden costs)*
— *how much time they spend reading and critiquing scripts*
— *if you can see a sample critique*
— *what is their screenwriting background*
— *how they were trained to analyze screenplays*
— *if they received a degree in writing or screenwriting*
— *were or are they studio or agency readers*
— *if they have taught screenwriting at a college or university*
— *will they do line editing*
— *what type and how much feedback will they give*
— *what kind and how much follow-up will you get*
— *if they can provide references from former clients*

If you have additional questions to ask, please do. Good readers will be happy to answer them. If they don't answer, hedge, act annoyed, are demeaning, or seem just plain bored, be leery. If you feel you're being pressured, take time to reassess. I am always more than suspicious of high-powered sales tactics.

Whichever person or group you choose, if they are conscientious, knowledgeable, and professional, you probably have what you need. Otherwise, it's best to cast your net elsewhere.

Critique Groups

Another avenue I urge you to explore is to form or join a *critique group*. Joining a group of other screenwriters who will listen and give you honest and constructive feedback is one of the most positive steps you can take to further your writing career.

A critique group is a cluster of friends or associates who help each other improve their writing and get it sold. Agreeing to share your work every week or two provides you with a deadline and an incentive to write and edit more of your script so it will be ready to present to the group. Receiving immediate feedback from a coterie of trained, like-minded individuals helps in many ways.

First, it reminds you that you are not the only person with wild-eyed dreams, and that there are others who support you and want to help. Second, fees, if any, are small, and may just involve bringing some food each week or hosting the group from time to time. Third, you receive immediate feedback from people with several different viewpoints. You can take what seems best and discard the rest. And finally, it gets you out among people, away from just you and the computer, and gives you some critical down time from the solitary task of writing.

To form or find a group, you can sometimes put free ads in your local paper. Library and college bulletin boards are helpful. Your state or local film commission or local library might know of or even host such groups in your area.

Joining a critique group means, of course, that you play by their rules. Forming your own means you and the membership must come to a consensus on how the group will work. But if you can find or form a group that meets regularly and that is knowledgeable about screenwriting, it can be the next best thing to having your own reader. It will also cost you a lot less money and give you a lot more satisfaction.

Contests

I consider screenwriting contests to be the bridge between screenplay honing and screenplay marketing. Several of them offer feedback on your script from one or more screenwriting professionals, and entering them will give you some idea of how your script(s) stack up against much of the competition.

Screenwriting contests also are an excellent introduction to marketing your script. No method for breaking into the film industry has helped my students more than contests. Many of my most successful students sold scripts because they placed well or placed first in one of the many screenwriting contests that are offered every year. Winning contests, even small ones, has become a catalyst for success in Hollywood.

When I began teaching, there were, to my knowledge, only three screenwriting contests. Today, there are several hundred. Many are good, honest, strong contests, where winning or placing in a high bracket can get you noticed. Contests often hook up with agents and producers who want to see the top screenplays from that particular competition. Some contests offer to fly you to Los Angeles or introduce you to various agents and producers. Some offer money as well as access to agents or producers. And others just offer the thrill of victory and the chance to be read by an agent or two.

With all these contests to choose from, deciding on which ones to enter requires that you do your homework. Yes, it's exciting to enter a big contest — one where you can win lots of money and Hollywood access — but it's also exciting for the three or four or five thousand other people who are entering. Certainly, enter the big ones but consider the smaller competitions as well.

Two of my students made their mark by winning an older but smaller contest. Their winning Tele-Play happened to be for a show on which the contest judge worked. Because that judge recommended them to the show's staff, they were asked to come out and pitch, which they did several times. Though they never actually sold an idea to that particular show, their pitch got them an agent, and the agent landed them a staff position on another show. All this because they entered not the largest or most glamorous of contests, but a small, well-respected one.

Not all contests are wonderful of course, and you should evaluate them carefully before you enter. Several on-line sites focus on screenwriting contests. They have lists, report cards, and bulletin boards where you can find good (and not-so-good) information about the various contests — history, price, winners, etc.

What should you look for when entering a contest? Price is certainly a factor. Some contests are terribly expensive, others more modest. Most contests need to charge something. After all, the contest has bookkeeping expenses, payment for readers, mailing, and other administrative costs. Still, extremely high prices — above or well above average — are, for me, an immediate red flag.

How the contest is conducted is important. Contests that ask you confidential information such as age, date of graduation, sex, etc., generally have an agenda. If the agenda is stated up front, then at least you know. For instance, a contest that asks for age because it's for those over forty or one that asks for race because it's for minorities is fine as long as the reason is printed on the entry form.

Another criterion to look for is *cold read*. In other words, has the entry form made it clear that the script will not give any personal information about the writer, such as name, sex, address, phone number, or email. I have seen contests that wanted this information for the reader. I don't think that is a decent or fair way to run a contest.

You might also look for contests that provide a critique. As I mentioned earlier, this is one way to receive some valuable feedback about your script that your editor or critique group may have missed.

Of course, it helps to know something about who is giving that feedback. If you can find out who the judges have been in the past (for obvious reasons, most contests won't reveal the judges they are using at present) it might clue you in to the kind of judges they are using now.

Screenwriting contests are one of the best ways of getting past the barriers thrown up around Hollywood. Winning or placing well in a contest may get your script noticed by agents and producers. It also means that someone with some credibility has pronounced your script producible, and that can be the e-ticket in Hollywood to go to the next, higher level.

Learning to write scripts, writing and receiving feedback, and taking those first steps such as entering contests are excellent ways to prepare yourself before diving into the nuts and bolts of the business of Hollywood.

Chapter 20
Hollywood Script Structure

The Hollywood Script Structure will take you where you want to go.

I'm glad you've bought this book. I hope it will help you achieve your ultimate goal of writing successful scripts for the film and television industry. I am sometimes asked, "Is the Hollywood Script Structure the only way to write successful screenplays?" It would be in my best interest to say, "Absolutely, otherwise no one in Hollywood is going to even give your script a second glance." But there are many ways to create and write screenplays. West Coast, East Coast, Character Driven, Non-linear, and Vignette Style come to mind. What I have discovered over my many years of teaching is that if you learn the basic guidelines and form for the most popular scripts and movies being produced today, you will be able to use that knowledge for any other type of script that you might want to write.

Screenwriting, like many other art forms, is fluid, and conventions that have been successful for more than thirty-five years are certain to have those who stray from them and find success. The bottom line is that it's all about good story telling, and agents and producers are always seeking good, compelling stories.

Even when you have that good, compelling story, getting it down on paper still can be a challenge. One element I always give a lot of points for when grading students is improvement. The goal is to continually improve each new or rewritten scene until the entire script shines. So yes, it may take books, courses, workshops, and many attempts before you and your script will be ready to take on Hollywood. And each rewrite you make will improve your work, each critique you receive will provide you with an opportunity to do that much better, and each improvement will bring you closer to the day when you're ready to send your script off to that contest, that agent, or that producer.

I hope you've enjoyed this book and learned from it. I hope your stories are clearer, your writing better, and your screenplays more producible than before you read it. Good luck with all your writing and all your scripts. I look forward to seeing your name up there on the movie screen and hearing it at the Oscars sometime in the not too distant future.

About The Author

Rick Reichman received an MFA in Professional Writing from the University of Southern California, and is a former winner of America's Best Screenwriting Competition. He worked as a coverage editor for Chuck Fries Productions in Los Angeles and as Head Writer for Willoughby Productions of Virginia, where he wrote several documentaries and industrial films. He recently optioned a co-written adaptation of the documentary "The Chain Gang."

In addition to being a veteran workshop instructor, Reichman has taught screenwriting classes to students at Georgetown University, American University, Tennessee State University, and the University of Virginia. His students have sold scripts to Fox, Warner Brothers, HBO, and Showtime, as well as to the television series' *Roseanne, Home Improvement, The Nanny, Xena—Warrior Princess, Buffy the Vampire Slayer, Family Law,* and most recently, *Crossing Jordan,* and *New Amsterdam.*

Reichman's first book, *Formatting Your Screenplay*, was a Writer's Digest Book Club alternate selection. His articles have appeared in several magazines including *Creative Screenwriting* and *The Writer*. He currently critiques scripts and teaches screenwriting at Santa Fe Community College in New Mexico.

Appendix A
Movies Mentioned in Book

1. 2001: A Space Odyssey
2. A Beautiful Mind
3. A Little Romance
4. A Thousand Clowns
5. Agnes of God
6. Airplane
7. Alice Doesn't Live Here Anymore
8. Aliens
9. Altered States
10. Americanization of Emily, The
11. Annie Hall
12. Aviator, The
13. Babe
14. Back to the Future
15. Beetle Juice
16. Beverly Hills Cop
17. Breaking Away
18. Bridges of Madison County
19. Buckaroo Banzai
20. Butch Cassidy and The Sundance Kid
21. Casablanca
22. Castaway
23. Chicago
24. Christine
25. Clash Of The Titans
26. Crying Game, The
27. Dave
28. Dead Poet's Society
29. Diva
30. Dogma

31. Dr. Jekyll and Mr. Hyde (Ibid)
32. E.T
33. Easy Rider
34. Enigma
35. Erin Borckovitch
36. Firm, The
37. First Blood
38. Forrest Gump
39. Friday the Thirteenth
40. Fugitive, The
41. Ghost
42. Godzilla vs. Bambi
43. Gone With The Wind
44. Groundhog Day
45. Halloween
46. Harley Davidson and the Marlboro Man
47. Harriet the Spy
48. Harry and Tonto
49. Hell's Angels
50. Herbie: The Love Bug
51. Honeymoon in Vegas
52. I Am Sam
53. Jaws
54. Kramer v. Kramer
55. Lethal Weapon
56. Little Big Man
57. Little Shop of Horrors
58. Lone Wolf McQuade
59. M*A*S*H
60. Marty
61. Mask, The
62. Matewan
63. Matrix, The
64. Men in Black
65. Mighty Aphrodite

66. Million Dollar Baby
67. Murphy's Romance
68. My Dinner With Andre
69. Network
70. Nightmare on Elm Street
71. Nutty Professor, The
72. Oh God
73. Oh God, You Devil
74. Ordinary People
75. Out of Africa
76. Perfect Storm, The
77. Princess Bride, The
78. Raiders of the Lost Ark
79. Return of the Secaucus Seven
80. Rocky
81. Romancing the Stone
82. Secret of My Success, The
83. Shakespeare In Love
84. Shindler's List
85. Sideways
86. Silence of the Lambs, The
87. Sixth Sense, The
88. Sleepless in Seattle
89. Star Wars
90. Steel Magnolias
91. Them
92. Tootsie
93. Top Gun
94. Toy Story
95. Turner and Hooch
96. Twelve Monkeys
97. War Games
98. War of the Roses, The
99. Witness
100. You Can Count On Me

Appendix B
Glossary

A-B Dialogue: A series of exercises that use your writing ability, your ear for language, your imagination, and even your acting skill to create compelling and realistic dialogue. (pg. 147)

Act Reversal: The point in the act at which the direction and emotion (secondary and primary) changes, taking the story in a different direction. (pg. 122)

Backstory: *Who*, *what*, and *why* and *how*. Who are these characters? What made them the type of people they are? How and why did they come to be where they are when our story opens? (pg. 35)

Baring the Soul: The point in your script where the protagonist speaks the truth about himself and/or his situation. (pg. 142)

Blah blah form: A formatting exercise in which a "b", "l", "a", and "h" is substituted for each letter on the original page of a screenplay. (pg. 58)

Bridging in: Opens your scene and consists of a *slug line* and the prose paragraph that follows. (pg. 25)

Bridging out: To exit the scene. (pg. 38)

Character Arc: A general plan for how your protagonist and other characters might change over the course of your story. (pg. 200)

Character Facade: A character's outward expression (clothes, speech pattern lifestyle, etc.) of inward change. This type of exterior evolution helps depict inner character transitions and gives audiences a clearer notion of how and why those adjustments occur. (pg. 200)

Character Cue: Begin dialogue paragraphs with the character cue, or speaker's name, in caps. (pg. 68)

Climax: The dramatic climax is the last real encounter between the protagonist and antagonist, and it usually appears just before the resolution in the third act. (pg. 143)

Conflict: The emotional tension needed to maintain an audience's interest. (pg. 27)

Connectives: Story devices that involve the repeating of objects, images, or phrases at different places in the script to represent change and to give a sense of completeness to the story. (pg. 169)

Contact Point: The point in the story at which a scene begins. (pg. 39)

Critique Service: An organization or individual that analyzes and reviews screenplays for a fee. (pg. 209)

Direction: Delineates the action in a screenplay and describes characters, settings, and objects. (pg. 67)

Discovery Tale: Type of screenplay in which one or more of the characters learns something about themselves or their histories by hearing or experiencing someone else's story. (pg. 174)

Ellipses: Time jumps that allow you to compress real time and concentrate only on the moments essential to the story. (pg. 171)

Ending: The ending provides the audience with evidence that the change in the protagonist is permanent. (pg. 139)

Exposition: Information that the audience must know in order to understand the scene. (pg. 134)

First Scene Reversal: The incident or event that pulls the protagonist from his original goal. (pg. 133)

Foreshadowing: Literally means to indicate or suggest beforehand. In your screenplay, foreshadowing is a sign of things going amiss, of plans — especially the protagonist's — going awry. (pg. 189)

Hero: The individual who triumphs over great odds, and pushes the action for more than half the screenplay. (pg. 94)

Low Point: the point in your screenplay where it seems that the hero, despite his valiant efforts, will be unable to succeed in his quest, and that nobility is all that he will be capable of achieving. (pg. 141)

Main Character: Always the hero. The character in the screenplay who drives the action for more than half the story. (pg. 94)

Marginals: In formatting, marginals denote the small but significant items found on the margins of the page. These items include, title, page numbers, *the end*, and *continued*. (pg. 72)

Middle-Act Reversal: The event in your screenplay that pulls the protagonist across a threshold and places her in a situation where she must adapt to a new and changing environment. (pg. 136)

Mise-en-scene: French word meaning *everything in the scene*. (pg. 34)

Normal Mode: What the protagonist's life is like the moment before the event that changes his destiny happens. (pg. 132)

Overture: The first few pages of the script written so that all the themes of the film are hinted at by the various visuals and/or dialogue of the characters. (pg. 20)

Pacing: Screenwriting device concerned with mastering the rhythms of the screenplay; it involves blending writing and format style into a page arrangement that enhances the story you depict with your words. (pg. 170)

Primary Emotion: The emotion portrayed by the characters in a screenplay. (pg. 13)

Resolution: The point or scene in which the protagonist either achieves his goal or is ennobled by the effort. (pg. 139)

Reversal: The point in a scene at which the action and/or emotion (secondary and primary) either takes a surprising twist or reaches an unexpected intensity. (pg. 41)

Rhyming: A story device that uses similarities to depict change and help an audience accept changes in characters, setting, and/or situations. (pg. 165)

Road Show: A type of screenplay where the main character is on a physical journey toward a goal or destination. (pg. 168)

Scene: A segment of your screenplay (usually between 3.5 to 7 pages long) centered on a theme and/or action and having a beginning, middle, climax, and end. (pg. 19)

Script Contact Point: Point at which the screenplay begins. (pg. 131)

Secondary Emotion: The emotion induced in the audience or reader. (pg. 14)

Screenwriting Contest: Competition that constitutes the bridge between screenplay honing and screenplay marketing. (pg. 212)

Sequence: Two or more scenes centered on a theme and/or action with a beginning, middle, and end. (pg. 71)

Set Up: A story device that acts as a red herring, misleading your audience as to where your scene is headed. (pg. 30)

Slug: An always capitalized formatting device that depicts the story setting and the time of day. (pg. 25)

Story Set Point: The turning point in your script where the main plot line becomes evident; it occurs somewhere around the middle of the first act. (pg. 135)

Subplot: Secondary stories that add depth and dimension to your script. Subplots crisscross the main plot line and help or hinder the protagonist in her effort to reach her goal. (pg. 173)

Subtext: The hidden meanings of conversations, actions, and decisions of the characters in the story. (pg. 175)

Talking Heads: Successive pages of dialogue with little or no action. (pg. 37)

Appendix C
Sample Screenplay

True Magic
by
Barbara Jacksha

"TRUE MAGIC"

FADE IN:

EXT. TRUCK STOP — DAY   (SUMMER, PRESENT)

A grungy truck stop stands at the edge of nowhere, New Mexico. Beyond it, there's only flat earth, scrubby sage, trash, and tumbleweeds.

TRUCK STOP PARKING LOT

In a far corner of the parking lot, an RV approaches a man who appears to sleep in a chair behind the table. A large, well-worn knapsack rests in the dust behind him.

TOO-TALL'S TABLE

The man is TOO-TALL. He's scruffy, sixties, looking possibly Native American. He dressed for the part. Medicine pouch. Heavy turquoise and silver jewelry. Beaded feather wand fluttering in his shirt pocket. Cowboy hat pulled low over his eyes.

The RVs engine RUMBLES, gravel CRUNCHES

     TOO-TALL
 Carmella?

Too-Tall opens his eyes to slits.

RV

A WOMAN hurries down the steps of the RV. A MAN reluctantly follows. Both are middle-aged, clueless, dressed in tourist garb more suited for Hawaii than dusty New Mexico.

TOO-TALL'S TABLE

Too-Tall closes his eyes again, pretends to sleep.

                      TOO-TALL
         Touristas.

RV

The woman straightens the man's collar. She fluffs her hair.

                      WOMAN
            That has to be Too-Tall.

                      MAN
            Too what?

                      WOMAN
            Too-Tall, the fortune teller. That
            nice clerk at the motel said he's
            from a line of medicine men going
            back six generations. Imagine!
            Let's have him read our fortune.

                      MAN
            Sure, whatever you want.

He pulls a camera from his shirt pocket.

                      WOMAN
            No, don't take his picture. It's
            important we respect their customs.
            And don't point. They don't like
            that either. I don't remember why.

The man looks toward the truck stop.

                      MAN
            Think it's safe to eat the food?

TOO-TALL'S TABLE

The tourists sit in unsteady folding chairs opposite Too-Tall, who slowly opens his eyes. He points to a hand-printed, cardboard sign anchored by a rock: "Hear your Future. $50."

>   MAN
>   Fifty dollars!

>   TOO-TALL
>   Powerful magic.

The man stands and walks toward the RV. The woman flashes a nervous smile, then hurries after him. They talk indistinctly.

Too-Tall pulls the feather wand from his pocket and taps it against his chin. He chants loudly.

TRUCK STOP PARKING LOT

A pick-up turns into the parking lot.

TOO-TALL'S TABLE

Still chanting, Too-Tall eyes the pick-up. The woman returns.

>   WOMAN
>   Sorry, we're new at this. Can you
>   tell me about my Sammy? He's just
>   not finding his place in life. . . .

TRUCK STOP

A Hispanic, twenty-something couple exits the pick-up. RANDY is handsome, athletic. CARMELLA is pretty, graceful. She carries a purse and is dressed in a waitress uniform with a "Carmella" name tag and a patch that matches the name of the truck stop.

>   CARMELLA
>   I'll be right in. I promised Too-Tall
>   some mints today.

She pulls a container of breath mints from her purse and rattles them playfully.

> RANDY
> My fiance likes hanging out with
> the strange man — should I be worried?

> CARMELLA
> Don't be silly, Randy.

Carmella kisses Randy on the cheek, then walks toward Too-Tall.

TOO TALL'S TABLE

Too-Tall moves the feather wand in elaborate motions while his eyelids flutter. He exhales deeply, points the feather wand at the woman's face.

> TOO-TALL
> No worries. All this life, you plant.
> Plant this, plant that.Now you reap
> the harvest.

Too-Tall lays down the wand. The woman clasps her hands.

> MAN
> That's it?

Too-Tall pushes the cardboard sign forward. The woman stands, pats her husbands arm.

> WOMAN
> Pay the man.

> MAN
> For what?

> WOMAN
> Oh for Pete's sake.

Carmella walks up behind the tourists. She watches the woman pull money from her purse and hand it to Too-Tall. He tucks it in his medicine pouch, then nods toward the truck stop.

                     TOO-TALL
             Be careful what you order.

Too-Tall suddenly finches. His hand flies to his forehead.

INSERT TOO-TALL'S VISION

In Too-Tall's vision, a train whistle BLOWS. The RV idles at the exit of the truck stop's parking lot. Randy's truck waits behind it. Randy HONKS his horn impatiently.

As the second train whistle BLOWS, the RV pulls out into traffic. Inside the RV, the tourists' expressions turn to horror. The woman throws her arms over her face and screams.

BACK TO SCENE

Too-Tall rubs his forehead. He clears his throat.

                     TOO-TALL
           Second whistle. You must stop.

Carmella's gaze snaps to Too-Tall. She frowns.

                     WOMAN
             Excuse me?

                     MAN
           Let's go. I'm hungry.

As the man steers the woman toward the truck stop, Too-Tall turns the cardboard sign over. This side reads: "Hear your Future. $10."

Carmella sits at the table. She slides the mints toward Too-Tall, who takes them and tucks them into his pocket. Carmella twists her engagement ring. Too-Tall taps the feather wand.

CARMELLA
What's that about a second whistle?

TOO-TALL
A warning from the spirits.

CARMELLA
They're full of stupid warnings, aren't they?

TOO-TALL
I'll read you again. No charge.

CARMELLA
After yesterday? I don't think so.

TOO-TALL
I only tell what the spirits show.

CARMELLA
But you're wrong. Randy is a good man. He's sweet and generous. He brings me cherry lifesavers every Saturday — just because we had them on our first date.

TOO-TALL
You asked the spirits if marrying him was the right thing. Why ask if you're not sure?

CARMELLA
For fun. Maybe to find out how many kids we'll have. Not to hear. . .

TOO-TALL
That he will beat you.

CARMELLA
He's not like that. Ask anyone.

TOO-TALL
I asked the spirits.

                    CARMELLA
          You must have heard them wrong.

Carmella rubs her belly. Too-Tall points it out.

                    TOO-TALL
          Ah, the doubt is stirring.

                    CARMELLA
          No! Everything's ready, everyone
          is so excited. You're the one who
          put all these terrible thoughts in
          my head. I mean, what am I
          supposed to do with them?

                    TOO-TALL
          Cancel the wedding.

Carmella slams her purse on the table.

                    CARMELLA
          Fine. Read me again. Let the
          spirits convince you I'm right.

Too-Tall studies her, then sets aside his feather wand.

                    TOO-TALL
          This time we use true magic.

Too-Tall pulls a rosary from his medicine pouch. The silver cross dangles like a pendulum.

INT. TRUCK STOP RESTAURANT

The seated tourists scan menus. A thirty-something Hispanic waitress approaches, order pad at the ready.

                    MAN
          I'll have the enchilada plate.

                    WOMAN
Are you sure? Too-Tall said to be
careful about what we ordered.

                    WAITRESS
He said that?

                    WOMAN
Yes, and I'm curious. What is he?
I bet he's a Navajo like in those
Hillerman books.

                    WAITRESS
I think he said his people come
from Cuba. Maybe it was France.

                    MAN
Definitely the enchilada plate.

REAR OF RESTAURANT

As the waitress nears the kitchen, she gets a quick kiss on the cheek from Randy who has stepped out of the men's room.

                    RANDY
Hola, beautiful.

                    WAITRESS
Look at you, the happy groom to be.

                    RANDY
Yeah, one more day. Can you grab
me a beer? Carmella's driving me
crazy. Talking non-stop about the
wedding. Yak, yak, yak. . . .

The waitress retrieves a beer. Randy takes a swallow.

                    WAITRESS
Where is Carmella? She's late.

                    RANDY
Out with Too-Tall.

                    WAITRESS
Again? You know, his kind usually
move on after a day or two. But
he stays. I think because of her.

                    RANDY
Carmella?

                    WAITRESS
He told me she looks like his
granddaughter. About the same age,
too. Poor thing was killed by a
drunk driver just last year.
Tragic when they die so young.

                    RANDY
What does he want from Carmella?

                    WAITRESS
Probably just a kind word. You
know she sees the good in everyone.

                    RANDY
Maybe I should talk to him.
Convince him to move along.

                    WAITRESS
Ai, he's harmless.

Randy drinks more beer.

EXT. TOO-TALL'S TABLE

Too-Tall sets the pendulum cross swinging forward and back.

                    CARMELLA
          Ask the spirits if I should marry
          Randy tomorrow. And I want the
          truth this time

Too-Tall watches Carmella as the rosary pendulum swings more broadly. Then he shuts his eyes and bows his head.

INSERT TOO-TALL'S VISION

There's a flash of movement, SHOUTING.

BACK TO SCENE

Too-Tall's eyes open. The rosary pendulum swings in a clearly clockwise circle.

                    TOO-TALL
          The spirits say "no."

                    CARMELLA
          Are the spirits making it swing
          like that — or are you? Do it again.

With a sigh, Too-Tall sets the pendulum swinging forward and back again. He bows his head. His eyes squeeze shut.

INSERT TOO-TALL'S VISION

Inside a dark room, voices are angry, indistinct, floating.

Randy is disheveled, drinking from a whisky bottle. Carmela lies on the floor, blouse torn, hair wild. When she tries to rise, Randy throws the bottle. Carmella covers her head.

Randy stands over her. Points a gun. He fires.

BACK TO SCENE

Too-Tall suddenly drops the rosary. Carmella jumps.

CARMELLA
What?

Too-Tall can barely form words. He rubs his forehead.

TOO-TALL
He's drinking.

CARMELLA
No way. His parents are alcoholics.
He doesn't touch the stuff.

TOO-TALL
He will. A little, then a lot.

Carmella stands. So does Too-Tall, in pain, leaning on the table.

TOO-TALL (CONT'D)
He'll kill you, and the baby.

Carmella stares, open-mouthed, fighting tears.

TOO-TALL (CONT'D)
The spirits don't lie.

CARMELLA
Forget it. Randy and I are getting
married, and we're going to be happy.
You and your spirits can go to hell.

Carmella stalks toward the truck stop. Too-Tall slumps down, defeated, staring at the rosary.

TOO-TALL
I know. But she doesn't believe
me. What else can I do?

He rubs his forehead, slowly closes his eyes.

INT. TRUCK STOP RESTAURANT

Using potholders, the waitress carries a heaping enchilada plate to the tourists. She holds the plate toward the man, but pauses and watches Randy open the door.

>   WAITRESS
>   If you get cold feet, call me.
>
>   RANDY
>   First thing.

As Randy leaves, the man grabs the plate firmly. He lets go quickly, shakes his hands.

>   MAN
>   Damn it!

Startled, the waitress drops the plate. Food splatters the tourists.

>   MAN (CONT'D)
>   Are you looking for a lawsuit?
>   Look at my hands!
>
>   WAITRESS
>   Our plates are hot.
>
>   MAN
>   Thanks for the warning.

The tourists leave, storming past Carmella as she walks in.

EXT. PARKING LOT

The tourists push past Randy and almost knock him down.

RV

Waiting near the RV, Too-Tall watches Randy check the tires on his truck. Too-Tall jiggles the mints Carmella gave him. When the tourists return, Too-Tall steps forward.

> TOO-TALL
> The spirits have more to tell you.

> MAN
> I've had enough for one day.

> WOMAN
> Yes, we really should get back.

Too-Tall watches Randy hop into his truck, then he looks back at the tourists climbing into the RV. He holds out the money the woman paid him earlier.

> TOO-TALL
> The spirits say that for you,
> everything is free.

This brings the tourists back. The man takes the cash.

> WOMAN
> What do the spirits want to say?

Too-Tall watches Randy's car back up, then pull away.

A train whistle BLOWS.

PARKING LOT EXIT

Randy waits at the exit for an oncoming car to pass by. His fingers drum the steering wheel.

A second whistle BLOWS. Randy floors the pick-up.

RV

Sounds of an accident: tires SQUEAL, horns BLARE, metal CRUNCHES.

> MAN
> My God.

> WOMAN
> What was that?

Too-Tall watches Carmella emerge from the truck stop and then run screaming toward the road.

Too-Tall runs a hand over his face, then turns to the tourists.

> TOO-TALL
> The spirits give you the rarest of
> gifts — a second chance. Use it well.

Too-Tall picks up his feather wand, hoists the knapsack onto his shoulder, then walks toward the middle of nowhere.

FADE OUT.

THE END

Appendix D
Suggested Reading List

Screenwriting Updated: New (and Conventional) Ways of Writing for the Screen, Linda Aronson, Silman-James Press; 1st Silman-James Ed, 2001

Poetics, Aristotle, Penguin Classics; New edition, 1997

The Craft of the Screenwriter, John Brady, J.C. Tarcher, New York, NY. 1992

The Hero With a Thousand Faces, Joseph Campbell, Princeton University Press; Reprint edition, Princeton, NJ. 1972

The Art of Dramatic Writing, Lajos Egri, Simon and Schuster, New York, NY. 1960

Screenplay, Syd Field, Dell Publishing, New York, NY. 1984

Selling a Screenplay: The Screenwriter's Guide to Hollywood, Syd Field, Dell Publishing, New York, NY. 1989

Adventures in the Screentrade, William Goldman, Warner Books, New York, NY. 1983

Hollywood Agents & Managers Directory, Hollywood Creative Directory, Santa Monica, CA. Yearly

Writing for Emotional Impact, Karl Iglesias, Wingspan Press, Livermore, CA. 2005

Figures of Speech - 60 Ways to Turn a Phrase, Arthur Quinn, Hermagoras Press, Davis, CA. 1993

Formatting Your Screenplay, Rick Reichman, Santa Fe, NM. 2007

Thinking in Pictures, John Sayles, Houghton Mifflin, Boston, MA. 1987

Making a Good Script Great, Linda Seger, Samuel French Trade, New York, NY. 1987

The Writer's Journey, Chris Vogler, Michael Wiese, Studio City, CA. 1992

Screenwriting, Richard Walter, Plume/New American Library, New York, NY. 1988

The Whole Picture, Richard Walter, Plume, New York, NY. 1997

Writer's Guide to Selling Your Screenplay, Cynthia Whitcomb, Watson-Guptill Publications, 2002

Critique Page

Yes, I critique screenplays and Tele Plays. What I offer in my critiques is

- At least twenty (20) pages of line editing for both grammar and format.
- At least 10 (10) single-spaced pages of critique.
- Follow-up questions by phone or email.
- Re-critique for half of the regular critique price.

If you're not sure or would like a kind of test drive, I will critique the first thirty (30) pages of your script for 40% off the full-script rate.

For prices, questions, or to find out more about my critiques or seminars, workshops, and conference appearances, contact me at (505) 984-2927 or email me at rick@20thingsbook.com

To get at 10% discount off the regular or test drive price, cut out the coupon below and send it in with the hard copy of your script.

Thanks, I look forward to hearing from you and reading and critiquing your screenplay.

Rick Reichman

TWENTY THINGS COUPON
10% OFF CRITIQUE PRICE FOR
THE READER OF THIS BOOK

----

www.ingramcontent.com/pod-product-compliance
Lightning Source LLC
Chambersburg PA
CBHW072334300426
44109CB00042B/1433